Special INTRODUC...

It's like getting 2 issues FREE!

Subscribe now to **Cooking at Home,**
the new recipe magazine from
Company's Coming, and you'll get:

- more delicious, kitchen-tested recipes
- more reliable, easy-to-follow recipes
- more helpful hints
- more color pictures

Plus *a cooking Q&A with Canada's
best-loved cookbook author
Jean Paré.*

**If you enjoy our cookbooks
you'll love our magazine.**

No Risk! If you're not completely
satisfied with *Cooking at Home,*
we'll refund you the entire cost of
your subscription.

Grant Lovig
Grant Lovig, Publisher

DETACH AND MAIL THIS CARD TODAY!
or call toll free 1-888-747-7171 and quote reference CBLPXCH.

SUBSCRIBE AND SAVE 33%

☑**YES!** Send me one year (6 issues) of *Cooking at Home*
for just $19.99 (plus taxes) – I'll save 33% off
the $29.94 cover price.

NAME _____
(Please Print)

ADDRESS _____ CITY _____

PROV/STATE _____ POSTAL CODE/ZIP _____

E-MAIL ADDRESS _____

○ Cheque payable to *Cooking at Home* enclosed.
○ Please bill me.
○ Charge my ○ VISA ○ MasterCard

ACCOUNT # _____ EXPIRY _____

CARDHOLDER SIGNATURE _____

PRICES OUTSIDE CANADA IN US FUNDS. PLEASE ALLOW UP TO 8 WEEKS FOR DELIVERY OF FIRST ISSUE.
ANNUAL NEWSTAND PRICE $29.94. INTRODUCTORY PRICE GUARANTEED THROUGH 2004.

YOU SAVE $10.00

CBLPXCH

From the name you trust most in recipes

Cooking at Home
CANADA'S OWN RECIPE MAGAZINE

Enjoy great new recipes delivered right to your door every 2 months!

SPECIAL INTRODUCTORY OFFER!

Complete the order form on the reverse and mail today. Or order on-line at www.companyscoming.com

SUBSCRIBE NOW!

6 RECIPE-PACKED ISSUES!

See over....

SAVE
33% NOW

1000008230-L3P8A7-BR01

Cooking at Home

```
SUBSCRIBER SERVICES
PO BOX 738 STN MAIN
MARKHAM ON   L3P 9Z9
```

The Beef Book

Jean Paré

www.**companys**coming.com
visit our web-site

Front Cover

1. Minty Beef Salad, page 102
2. Meatball Vegetable Soup, page 117
3. Barbecued Beef Ribs, page 39
4. Rolled Steak Florentine, page 66
5. Sesame Kabobs With Spinach, page 62

Props Courtesy Of:
  Treasure Barrel
  X/S Wares

Back Cover

1. Beer Burgers, page 30
2. Taco Cheese Burgers, page 33

Props Courtesy Of:
  The Bay

Now in Original Series

The Beef Book contains 140 choice recipes selected from Company's Coming *Beef Today!*

Our special thanks to the Beef Information Centre for permission to use selected recipes.

The Beef Book
Copyright © Company's Coming Publishing Limited
All rights reserved worldwide. No part of this book may be reproduced in any form by any means without written permission in advance from the publisher. Brief portions of this book may be reproduced for review purposes, provided credit is given to the source. Reviewers are invited to contact the publisher for additional information.

First Printing February 2002

Canadian Cataloguing in Publication Data

Paré, Jean
    The beef book
(Original Series)
Includes index.
Previously published under title: Beef today!
ISBN 1-895455-81-2

    1. Cookery (Beef) I. Title. II. Title: Beef today!. III. Series:
Paré, Jean. Original series.

TX749.5.B43P368 2002   641.6'62   C2001-901923-8

Published by
COMPANY'S COMING PUBLISHING LIMITED
2311 - 96 Street
Edmonton, Alberta, Canada T6N 1G3
Tel: (780) 450-6223   Fax: (780) 450-1857
www.companyscoming.com

Company's Coming is a registered trademark owned by Company's Coming Publishing Limited

Printed in Canada

Cooking Tonight?
Drop by companyscoming.com

companyscoming.com

| Who We Are | Browse Cookbooks | Cooking Tonight? | Home |

everyday ingredients

feature recipes

feature recipes — Cooking tonight? Check out this month's **feature recipes**—absolutely FREE!

tips and tricks — Looking for some great kitchen helpers? **tips and tricks** is here to save the day!

reader circle — In search of answers to cooking or household questions? Do you have answers you'd like to share? Join the fun with **reader circle**, our on-line question and answer bulletin board. Our **reader circle chat room** connects you with cooks from around the world. Great for swapping recipes too!

cooking links — Other interesting and informative web-sites are just a click away with **cooking links.**

cookbook search — Find cookbooks by title, description or food category using **cookbook search**.

contact us — We want to hear from you—**contact us** lets you offer suggestions for upcoming titles, or share your favorite recipes.

Company's Coming
COOKBOOKS

everyday recipes trusted by millions

Company's Coming Cookbooks

Original Series

- 150 Delicious Squares
- Casseroles
- Muffins & More
- Salads
- Appetizers
- Desserts
- Soups & Sandwiches
- Cookies
- Vegetables
- Main Courses
- Pasta
- Cakes
- Barbecues

- Pies
- Light Recipes
- Preserves
- Light Casseroles
- Chicken
- Kids Cooking
- Breads
- Meatless Cooking
- Cooking For Two
- Breakfasts & Brunches
- Slow Cooker Recipes
- Pizza
- One Dish Meals

- Starters
- Stir-Fry
- Make-Ahead Meals
- The Potato Book
- Low-Fat Cooking
- Low-Fat Pasta
- Appliance Cooking
- Cook For Kids
- Stews, Chilies & Chowders
- Fondues
- The Beef Book
- Asian Cooking **NEW**
  March 1/02

Greatest Hits Series

- Biscuits, Muffins & Loaves
- Dips, Spreads & Dressings
- Soups & Salads
- Sandwiches & Wraps
- Italian
- Mexican

Lifestyle Series

- Grilling
- Diabetic Cooking

Special Occasion Series

- Chocolate Everything
- Gifts from the Kitchen
- Cooking for the Seasons **NEW** *April 1/02*

Table of Contents

Foreword

Beef Cuts

Appetizers

Roasts

Soups

Stir-Frys

Reader Survey

The Company's Coming Story

Jean Paré grew up understanding that the combination of family, friends and home cooking is the essence of a good life. From her mother she learned to appreciate good cooking, while her father praised even her earliest attempts. When she left home she took with her many acquired family recipes, a love of cooking and an intriguing desire to read recipe books like novels!

"never share a recipe you wouldn't use yourself"

In 1963, when her four children had all reached school age, Jean volunteered to cater the 50th anniversary of the Vermilion School of Agriculture, now Lakeland College. Working out of her home, Jean prepared a dinner for over 1000 people which launched a flourishing catering operation that continued for over eighteen years. During that time she was provided with countless opportunities to test new ideas with immediate feedback—resulting in empty plates and contented customers! Whether preparing cocktail sandwiches for a house party or serving a hot meal for 1500 people, Jean Paré earned a reputation for good food, courteous service and reasonable prices.

"Why don't you write a cookbook?" Time and again, as requests for her recipes mounted, Jean was asked that question. Jean's response was to team up with her son, Grant Lovig, in the fall of 1980 to form Company's Coming Publishing Limited. April 14, 1981, marked the debut of "150 DELICIOUS SQUARES", the first Company's Coming cookbook in what soon would become Canada's most popular cookbook series.

Jean Paré's operation has grown steadily from the early days of working out of a spare bedroom in her home. Full-time staff includes marketing personnel located in major cities across Canada. Home Office is based in Edmonton, Alberta in a modern building constructed specially for the company.

Today the company distributes throughout Canada and the United States in addition to numerous overseas markets, all under the guidance of Jean's daughter, Gail Lovig. Best-sellers many times over in English, Company's Coming cookbooks have also been published in French and Spanish. Familiar and trusted in home kitchens around the world, Company's Coming cookbooks are offered in a variety of formats, including the original softcover series.

Jean Paré's approach to cooking has always called for quick and easy recipes using everyday ingredients. Even when traveling, she is constantly on the lookout for new ideas to share with her readers. At home, she can usually be found researching and writing recipes, or working in the company's test kitchen. Jean continues to gain new supporters by adhering to what she calls "the golden rule of cooking": never share a recipe you wouldn't use yourself. It's an approach that works—*millions of times over!*

Foreword

Beef has been a staple in North American diets for well over a century. Today's beef production has been adapted to our more health-conscious lifestyles. It is leaner, lower in cholesterol and is still one of the best sources of protein and iron. Beef is available in a wider variety of cuts than ever before. That's good news for busy, on-the-go individuals and families who demand the convenience of ready-to-cook meats.

Included in this book are contemporary and traditional favorite recipes. Why do Spaghetti Meat Sauce, Classic Meatloaf and Hearty Beef Stew continue to be a part of today's mealtime? Simply because they are easy to prepare using leaner beef, fresh ingredients and less cooking oil, and they maintain a satisfying flavor and pleasing texture.

While maintaining the Company's Coming tradition of creating quick and easy recipes, we find that most pre-packaged or prepared items are easily substituted using ingredients already in your kitchen. A simple alternative—using canned tomato sauce, or even canned tomatoes mixed with some herbs and spices— makes a tasty substitute for ketchup, saving loads of calories in the process.

We are careful to watch the amount of beef allocated per serving. The cuts of beef we chose are generally boneless and well-trimmed, resulting in less waste. Today's recommended serving is 3 to 3 1/2 oz. (85 to 100 g) of cooked beef (or 4 oz., 113 g, uncooked) per person. This is a good average on which to base the number of servings.

Let the *Beef Cuts Substitution Chart*, page 9, the *Roasting Guide*, page 11, and the *Recipe Index*, pages 153 to 156, help you plan meals. Flavorful, versatile and healthy, today's beef is featured at its delicious best in over 140 recipes. Whatever you choose, be it appetizer or soup, barbecue or stir-fry, for entertaining or everyday cooking, make it *The Beef Book*.

Jean Paré

Each recipe has been analyzed using the most up-to-date version of the Canadian Nutrient File from Health Canada, which is based upon the United States Department of Agriculture (USDA) Nutrient Data Base.

Margaret Ng, B.Sc. (Hon), M.A.
Registered Dietitian

Beef is Good for You!

Lean beef continues to be a major dietary source of protein, iron, zinc and the family of B vitamins. Protein found in beef is a "complete" protein made up of all the essential amino acids that the body must have for good health but cannot make itself. A good store of iron helps keep us alert, energetic and healthy. Zinc is a component of every living cell in the body. It is essential for growth and reproduction, night vision, digestion and appetite (enhancing our sense of taste and smell). Zinc is critical for maintaining the body's immune system and healing process. B vitamins regulate the many chemical reactions in the body necessary to promote growth and maintain health. Some help to release energy, some help to maintain good vision and healthy skin, and others are involved in the manufacture of red blood cells.

Trimming the Fat

Today's lean cuts of beef are trimmed to 1/4 inch (6 mm) or less of fat. Regular ground beef has a maximum fat content of 30%, lean a maximum of 17% and extra lean no more than 10%.

To reduce fat further, use a vegetable spray in place of butter, margarine or oil when browning beef. Or brown in the oven. Substitute low-fat or non-fat products for regular dairy products such as sour cream and cream cheese.

Safe Handling of Beef

1. Refrigerate raw beef at 32°F to 40°F (0°C to 4°C) for up to 4 days, ground beef for up to 2 days.

2. Place wrapped raw beef in a shallow dish in the refrigerator to safeguard against leaking onto other foods.

3. Keep vacuum-packed beef sealed and refrigerated or frozen until ready to use.

4. Cover and refrigerate leftover cooked beef within 1 hour.

5. Store leftover cooked beef tightly wrapped in the refrigerator for up to 7 days, or in the freezer for up to 3 months.

6. Cover and refrigerate beef sandwiches for no more than 24 hours and serve chilled to prevent spoilage.

7. Larger pieces of beef (raw or cooked) keep longer chilled or frozen than smaller cuts or cut-up beef.

8. Freeze raw beef in its original packaging for up to 2 weeks. For longer periods (up to 6 months), re-wrap beef in freezer-safe plastic film, heavy-duty aluminum foil or freezer paper. Do not re-freeze raw beef once it has been thawed.

Too Pink or Not Too Pink...

Should contamination occur, it will affect the surface of beef. Once roasts, steaks, cubes or strips have been browned on all sides, bacteria has been destroyed. Any red or pink beef inside will be safe to ingest. Ground beef, on the other hand, has bacteria throughout and should be cooked until no pink remains and juices are clear.

Beef Cuts

The degree of tenderness of a particular cut of beef depends on what part of the animal it comes from. Cuts from active muscle areas—the shoulders, flank and hips (or chuck; hip or round; brisket; plate or short plate)—are naturally less tender and leaner. The meat along the backbone—the ribs and loin or short loin—is the most tender.

Beef Cuts Substitution Chart

The chart below is intended as a guide to help you substitute one cut of beef for another in a recipe. For best results, it is recommended you stay within the same tenderness grouping in order to maintain the best cooking method. The *Roasting Guide*, page 11, can help you if you decide to substitute a cut of beef with a different degree of tenderness.

	Roasts	Steaks	Other
Tender (Rib, Loin, Short Loin, Sirloin)	Prime Rib, Rib Sirloin, Top Sirloin Standing Rib, Rib Tenderloin	Prime Rib, Rib Rib-Eye Sirloin, Top Sirloin Strip Loin Tenderloin T-Bone Wing	Back Ribs
Medium-Tender (Chuck, Hip, Round)	Shoulder Pot Cross-Rib (all cuts) Rump Sirloin Tip, Tip Blade (all cuts) Round (all cuts) 7-Bone Pot	Blade Round (all cuts) Cross-Rib Sirloin Tip, Tip	Ground Beef
Less Tender (Brisket, Shank, Flank, Plate, Short Plate)	Brisket Point Corned Brisket	Flank Short Rib	Short Ribs Shank Cross-Cut Stew Beef

Cooking Methods for Beef

There are two main methods for cooking beef—dry heat (roasting, broiling/grilling, barbecuing, frying, stir-frying) and moist heat (braising, stewing, pot roasting). The dry heat method is done without adding liquid; the moist heat method requires enough added liquid to keep the beef moist and help tenderize it during the cooking process.

Dry Heat Methods

Roasting: Best for tender roasts. Season as desired. Place, fat side up (if any), on a rack in an open roaster. Roast, uncovered, using the *Roasting Guide*, page 11.

Broiling: Best for tender steaks or medium-tender steaks if marinated beforehand. Place on a broiler rack 4 to 5 inches (10 to 12.5 cm) from the heat source. Broil using the *Roasting Guide*, page 11.

Barbecuing (Grilling): Best for tender roasts and steaks, ground beef patties, and for medium-tender roasts and steaks if marinated beforehand. Place 4 to 5 inches (10 to 12.5 cm) above the heat source. Barbecue using the *Roasting Guide*, page 11.

Indirect Barbecuing: Best for medium-tender roasts and steaks if marinated beforehand. Heat the barbecue on one side only. Place beef on unheated side of grill, or move coals from directly under beef. Barbecue using the *Roasting Guide*, page 11.

Frying: Best for tender steaks or medium-tender steaks if marinated beforehand. Season as desired. Preheat a non-stick frying pan on medium using little or no oil. Fry beef on both sides. Refer to the *Roasting Guide*, page 11.

Stir-Frying: Best for tender steak strips or medium-tender steaks if marinated beforehand. Preheat a non-stick frying pan or wok on high using little or no oil. Brown strips as quickly as possible, turning continuously.

Moist Heat Methods

Marinating or cooking in a mixture containing a food acid such as vinegar, lemon juice or wine will help to break down less tender muscle (connective) tissues. Liquid added can be water, broth, consommé, diluted soup, wine, etc.

Pot Roasting: Best for less tender roasts. Roast may or may not be coated with seasoned flour. Brown the roast on all sides, using little or no oil. Cover with liquid and cook, covered, according to the recipe being used.

Braising: Best for medium-tender roasts or steaks. For basic roasting, brown roast in a very hot preheated oven, then add 1 cup (250 mL) liquid. Cook, uncovered, using the *Roasting Guide*, below. For variations, cook according to the recipe being used. For steaks, brown in a non-stick frying pan on medium using little or no oil. Pour off any excess drippings. Add liquid and cook according to the recipe being used.

Stewing: Best for less tender roasts or steaks. Beef is cut into cubes or strips and may or may not be coated with flour, depending on the recipe. Brown in either a non-stick frying pan on medium using little or no oil or in an ungreased pan in a 350°F (175°C) oven. Place in a roasting pan, large saucepan or heatproof Dutch oven. Add liquid and cook, covered, according to the recipe directions.

Roasting Guide

Tenderness	Oven Temperature	Time*		Internal Temperature
Tender	325°F (160°C)	Rare	20min./lb. (45min./kg)	140°F (60°C)
		Medium	25min./lb. (55min./kg)	160°F (70°C)
		Well	30min./lb. (65min./kg)	170°F (75°C)
Medium-Tender	Step 1. 500°F (260°C)	30 minutes total		
	Step 2. (Add liquid)	1 1/4 - 1 3/4 hours total		160°F (70°C)
		275°F (140°C)		(2-5 lb., 1-2.5 kg)

*Cooking times are based on beef that has been completely thawed. If the roast is frozen, allow about 50% more cooking time. If there is any possibility that the core might still be frozen, insert a small skewer to test. If so, allow extra cooking time and continue to monitor doneness with meat thermometer.

Broiling/Grilling Guide**

Thickness	Minutes per Side		
	Rare	Medium	Well-Done
½-¾ inch (1-2 cm)	2 - 4	5 - 7	7 - 9
1 inch (2.5 cm)	4 - 8	7 - 10	9 -15
1½ inches (3.8 cm)	7 - 9	8 - 11	10 - 15
2 inches (5 cm)	8 - 14	15 - 20	25 - 30

** Broiling/Grilling times vary depending on distance from heat source, temperature of heat source and the cut of beef. Boneless steaks take less time than bone-in and tender cuts take less time than less tender cuts.

Herb Cheese Spread

Spread this on baguettes or fresh bread slices and serve with steak.

Chopped fresh chives	1 tbsp.	15 mL
Finely chopped fresh sweet basil	1 tsp.	5 mL
Crushed whole green peppercorns	1/4 tsp.	1 mL
Light cream cheese	4 oz.	125 g

Combine chives, basil and peppercorn in shallow bowl.

Shape cream cheese into 6 balls. Roll in herb mixture. Arrange on small plate. Cover. Chill. Remove from refrigerator 20 to 30 minutes before serving. Makes 6 balls.

1 ball: 48 Calories; 1.2 g Total Fat; 145 mg Sodium; 2 g Protein; 1 g Carbohydrate; trace Dietary Fiber

Pictured on page 17.

Brandy Pepper Sauce

A warm, rich, golden sauce with strong brandy and pepper accents.

Coarsely ground whole mixed peppercorns	1 tbsp.	15 mL
Finely chopped shallots (or green onion)	1 tbsp.	15 mL
Butter (not margarine)	1/4 cup	60 mL
Olive (or cooking) oil	1 tsp.	5 mL
Brandy	1/4 cup	60 mL
Condensed beef broth	3/4 cup	175 mL
Whipping cream	1/4 cup	60 mL

Sauté peppercorn and shallots in butter and olive oil in non-stick frying pan until shallots are soft.

Add brandy and broth. Bring to a boil. Boil, stirring occasionally, until reduced by half.

Stir in whipping cream. Bring to a boil. Boil for 2 minutes. Makes 1/2 cup (125 mL).

2 tsp. (10 mL): 68 Calories; 5.7 g Total Fat; 116 mg Sodium; 1 g Protein; 1 g Carbohydrate; trace Dietary Fiber

Pictured on page 17.

Roasted Peppers

Roast as many peppers, in as many different colors as you like. Use with Roasted Pepper And Beef Triangles, page 24; Beef And Rice Quiche, page 58; Goulash With Roasted Pepper, page 67; Oriental Stuffed Meatloaf, page 68.

Medium green (or red, orange or yellow) pepper	1	1

Place pepper over high heat on barbecue, on rack under broiler or, using tongs, directly on burner (gas is best) on high. Roast pepper until skin is blistered and blackened in places. Place in paper bag and close, or place in bowl and cover with plastic wrap. Let sweat for 15 minutes until cool enough to handle. Remove and discard skin. Remove seeds and membranes. Cut according to recipe directions.

1 pepper: 20 Calories; 0.1 g Total Fat; 1 mg Sodium; 1 g Protein; 5 g Carbohydrate; 0 g Dietary Fiber

Béarnaise Sauce

A slightly peppery version of the classic French recipe. Serve with Beef Benedict, page 104 or Pepper Steak For Two, page 123.

Finely chopped shallots (or green onion)	1 tbsp.	15 mL
Dried tarragon leaves, crushed	1 tsp.	5 mL
White pepper	1/8 tsp.	0.5 mL
Dry white (or alcohol-free) wine	1/2 cup	125 mL
White wine vinegar	1 tbsp.	15 mL
Egg yolks (large)	2	2
Hard margarine (or butter), melted	1/4 cup	60 mL
Cayenne pepper, dash		
Finely chopped fresh parsley (or 1/4 tsp., 1 mL, flakes)	1 tsp.	5 mL

Combine first 5 ingredients in small saucepan. Bring to a boil. Reduce heat. Simmer, uncovered, for 8 to 10 minutes until liquid is reduced to 1/3 cup (75 mL). Strain into small cup, discarding shallots.

Lightly whisk egg yolks in top of double boiler. Add 1 tbsp. (15 mL) melted margarine. Whisk. Place over barely simmering water. Whisk in wine mixture and remaining margarine. Whisk until fluffy and thickened. Remove from heat.

Add cayenne pepper and parsley. Stir. Makes 3/4 cup (175 mL).

2 tbsp. (30 mL): 49 Calories; 4.3 g Total Fat; 42 mg Sodium; 1 g Protein; 1 g Carbohydrate; trace Dietary Fiber

Aïoli Sauce

A garlic mayonnaise from Provence, France.
Serve with warm or cold Spanish Sirloin, page 32.

Garlic cloves, chopped (or 3/4 tsp., 4 mL, powder)	3	3
Salt	1/4 tsp.	1 mL
Lemon juice	1 tbsp.	15 mL
Large egg	1	1
Olive (or cooking) oil	1 cup	250 mL

Place garlic, salt, lemon juice and egg in blender or food processor. Process until creamy.

With motor running, slowly pour olive oil through hole in lid or through feed chute. Process until thick. Chill. Makes 1 cup (250 mL).

1 tbsp. (15 mL): 132 Calories; 14.6 g Total Fat; 46 mg Sodium; trace Protein; trace Carbohydrate; trace Dietary Fiber

Pineapple Salsa

Sweet and a little spicy, perfect served with Holiday Steak, page 32.

Can of pineapple tidbits, drained	8 oz.	227 mL
Chopped red onion	1/2 cup	125 mL
Chopped fresh cilantro (or fresh parsley)	2 tbsp.	30 mL
Lime juice	1 tbsp.	15 mL
Cayenne pepper	1/2 tsp.	2 mL

Combine all 5 ingredients in small bowl. Cover. Chill for at least 1 hour to blend flavors. Makes 1 1/8 cups (280 mL).

2 tbsp. (30 mL): 13 Calories; 0.5 g Total Fat; 1 mg Sodium; trace Protein; 3 g Carbohydrate; trace Dietary Fiber

Pictured on page 17.

 To make meatballs that are uniform in size, use a mini ice-cream scoop. Scoops are available in grocery and retail stores.

Fresh Tomato Salsa

Serve with, or spoon over, Pesto Meatloaf Roll, page 70.

Roma (plum) tomatoes, seeded and finely chopped	5	5
Olive (or cooking) oil	2 tbsp.	30 mL
Chopped fresh sweet basil	1 tbsp.	15 mL
Chopped fresh parsley (or 3/4 tsp., 4 mL, flakes)	1 tbsp.	15 mL
Garlic clove, minced (or 1/4 tsp., 1 mL, powder)	1	1
Salt	1 tsp.	5 mL

Combine all 6 ingredients in medium bowl. Cover. Chill for 2 hours to blend flavors. Makes 2 cups (500 mL).

2 tbsp. (30 mL): 24 Calories; 1.8 g Total Fat; 173 mg Sodium; trace Protein; 2 g Carbohydrate; trace Dietary Fiber

Salsa Romesco

Try this sauce over noodles or serve with Pepper Steak For Two, page 123.

Slivered almonds	1/4 cup	60 mL
Garlic clove, chopped (or 1/4 tsp., 1 mL, powder)	1	1
Cayenne pepper	1/4 tsp.	1 mL
Salt	1/2 tsp.	2 mL
Small tomato, peeled, seeded and chopped	1	1
Red wine vinegar	1/4 cup	60 mL
Chopped fresh parsley (or 3/4 tsp., 4 mL, flakes)	1 tbsp.	15 mL
Olive (or cooking) oil	3/4 cup	175 mL

Place almonds, garlic, cayenne pepper, salt, tomato, vinegar and parsley in blender or food processor. Purée.

With motor running, slowly pour olive oil through hole in lid or through feed chute. Process until thick. Chill. Makes 1 cup (250 mL).

2 tbsp. (30 mL): 205 Calories; 22.1 g Total Fat; 172 mg Sodium; 1 g Protein; 2 g Carbohydrate; trace Dietary Fiber

Black Bean Salsa

Make a day ahead to allow flavors to blend. Use in Barbecued Fajitas, page 29.

Can of black beans, with liquid	19 oz.	540 mL
Cayenne pepper	1/4 tsp.	1 mL
Salt	1/4 tsp.	1 mL
Garlic clove, minced (or 1/4 tsp., 1 mL, powder)	1	1
Lime juice	1 tsp.	5 mL
Chili powder	1/2 tsp.	2 mL
Finely chopped red onion	1/2 cup	125 mL
Red Roasted Pepper, page 13, cut into slivers	1	1
Finely chopped fresh cilantro (or fresh parsley)	1 tbsp.	15 mL
Medium tomato, seeded and diced	1	1
Ripe pitted whole olives, sliced	10	10

Combine first 6 ingredients in large saucepan. Bring to a boil on medium. Reduce heat to medium-low. Simmer for 15 minutes, stirring often to prevent scorching, until some liquid has evaporated and beans are soft. Remove from heat.

Add remaining 5 ingredients. Mix well. Chill. Makes 2 cups (500 mL).

2 tbsp. (30 mL): 30 Calories; 0.4 g Total Fat; 92 mg Sodium; 2 g Protein; 5 g Carbohydrate; 1 g Dietary Fiber

Pictured on page 17.

1. Pineapple Salsa, page 14
2. Brandy Pepper Sauce, page 12
3. Herb Cheese Spread, page 12
4. Black Bean Salsa, page 16

Props Courtesy Of: Off The Wall Gallery
Western Marble

Roasted Garlic Spread

Use as a spread for sandwiches or as a dip for veggies.

Large garlic bulb	1	1
Part-skim ricotta cheese	1/2 cup	125 mL
Non-fat sour cream	1/2 cup	125 mL
Salt	1/8 tsp.	0.5 mL
White pepper, dash		

Wrap garlic bulb in foil. Bake in 375°F (190°C) oven for 1 hour. Remove from oven. Cool in foil until able to handle. Remove foil. Cut off root end, exposing inside cloves. Squeeze cloves out of skins into small bowl. Mash with fork.

Add ricotta cheese, sour cream, salt and pepper. Mix well. Cover. Chill. Makes 1 cup (250 mL).

1 tbsp. (15 mL): 13 Calories; 0.6 g Total Fat; 34 mg Sodium; 1 g Protein; 1 g Carbohydrate; trace Dietary Fiber

1. Refried Bean Dip, page 23
2. Mexican Snackies, page 26

Props Courtesy Of: Chintz & Company

Spanish Meatballs

These delightful meatballs have a slight taste of wine and cloves.

MEATBALLS

Lean ground beef	1 lb.	454 g
Fresh whole wheat bread crumbs	1 cup	250 mL
Milk	2 tbsp.	30 mL
Large egg, fork-beaten	1	1
Garlic clove, minced (or 1/4 tsp., 1 mL, powder)	1	1
Salt	1/4 tsp.	1 mL
Pepper	1/4 tsp.	1 mL

SPANISH SAUCE

Medium onion, finely chopped	1	1
Garlic cloves, minced (or 1/2 tsp., 2 mL, powder)	2	2
Olive (or cooking) oil	1 tbsp.	15 mL
Beef bouillon powder	1/2 tsp.	2 mL
Boiling water	1/2 cup	125 mL
Tomato paste	1 tbsp.	15 mL
White (or alcohol-free) wine	1/2 cup	125 mL
Cornstarch	2 tsp.	10 mL
Pepper	1/4 tsp.	1 mL
Ground cloves	1/8 tsp.	0.5 mL
Brown sugar, packed	1 tsp.	5 mL

Meatballs: Combine all 7 ingredients in large bowl. Mix well. Shape into 1 inch (2.5 cm) balls. Place on ungreased baking sheet. Bake in 350°F (175°C) oven for 10 minutes until browned and no longer pink inside. Drain. Set aside.

Spanish Sauce: Sauté onion and garlic in olive oil in medium saucepan for 2 to 3 minutes until soft.

Dissolve bouillon powder in boiling water in small cup. Add to onion mixture. Stir. Add tomato paste. Stir.

(continued on next page)

Appetizers

Stir wine into cornstarch in small cup until smooth. Gradually stir into tomato paste mixture. Heat and stir until boiling and thickened.

Add pepper, cloves and brown sugar. Stir. Add meatballs. Heat on low for 25 to 30 minutes until heated through. Makes 36 meatballs.

1 meatball: 34 Calories; 1.6 g Total Fat; 42 mg Sodium; 3 g Protein; 1 g Carbohydrate; trace Dietary Fiber

Oriental Mini Beef Skewers

This lovely appetizer practically melts in your mouth!

Round (or flank) steak	1 lb.	454 g
MARINADE		
Cooking oil	1 tbsp.	15 mL
Liquid honey	1 tbsp.	15 mL
Sherry (or alcohol-free sherry)	1/4 cup	60 mL
Soy sauce	1/4 cup	60 mL
Garlic clove, minced (or 1/4 tsp., 1 mL, powder)	1	1
Finely grated gingerroot (or 1/4 tsp., 1 mL, ground ginger)	1 tsp.	5 mL
Green onion, chopped	1	1
Sesame seeds	2 tsp.	10 mL
Bamboo skewers, 4 inch (10 cm) length, soaked in water for 10 minutes	48	48

Slice steak diagonally across grain into 1/8 inch (3 mm) thick strips.

Marinade: Combine first 8 ingredients in large bowl. Stir well. Place beef strips in shallow dish or resealable freezer bag. Pour marinade over beef. Stir or turn to coat. Cover or seal. Marinate in refrigerator for 4 hours or overnight, stirring or turning several times. Remove beef. Discard marinade.

Thread beef strips, accordion-style, onto skewers. Broil for about 2 minutes per side until desired doneness. Makes 48 skewers.

1 skewer: 12 Calories; 0.4 g Total Fat; 26 mg Sodium; 2 g Protein; trace Carbohydrate; trace Dietary Fiber

Beef Jerky

An old time favorite snack, homemade.

Soy sauce	1/4 cup	60 mL
Brown sugar, packed	2 tbsp.	30 mL
Worcestershire sauce	1 tbsp.	15 mL
Ground ginger	1/2 tsp.	2 mL
Salt	1/2 tsp.	2 mL
Pepper	1/8 tsp.	0.5 mL
Lean flank (or top round or sirloin tip) steak, cut into 1/4 inch (6 mm) thick strips	1 lb.	454 g

Combine first 6 ingredients in small bowl.

Place beef strips in shallow dish or resealable freezer bag. Pour marinade over beef. Stir or turn to coat. Cover or seal. Marinate in refrigerator for 6 to 12 hours, turning several times. Remove beef. Discard marinade. Place wire rack on baking sheet. Arrange beef strips in single layer on rack. Bake in 175°F (80°C) oven for about 8 hours until beef is dried. Store in airtight container in refrigerator or freeze for long-term storage. Makes 1/2 lb. (225 g).

1/2 lb. (225 g): 649 Calories; 24.6 g Total Fat; 1598 mg Sodium; 92 g Protein; 9 g Carbohydrate; trace Dietary Fiber

Hot Cheese Rounds

Make ahead and freeze. No need to reheat—just bring to room temperature.

Lean ground beef	3/4 lb.	340 g
Salt	1/2 tsp.	2 mL
Cayenne pepper	1/4 tsp.	1 mL
All-purpose flour	1 1/2 cups	375 mL
Baking powder	1 tbsp.	15 mL
Hard margarine (or butter)	3 tbsp.	50 mL
Grated sharp Cheddar cheese	1 cup	250 mL
Finely chopped green onion	1/4 cup	60 mL
Worcestershire sauce	1 tsp.	5 mL
Beef bouillon powder	1 tsp.	5 mL
Boiling water	1/3 cup	75 mL
Paprika	1/8 tsp.	0.5 mL

(continued on next page)

Appetizers

Scramble-fry ground beef, salt and cayenne pepper in non-stick frying pan until beef is no longer pink. Drain well. Cool slightly.

Combine flour and baking powder in large bowl. Cut in margarine until crumbly. Add cheese, green onion and beef mixture. Stir.

Combine Worcestershire sauce, bouillon powder and boiling water in small cup. Add to beef mixture. Mix well. Shape into 1 inch (2.5 cm) balls. Place on lightly greased baking sheet. Press balls down with fork. Sprinkle with paprika. Bake in 400°F (205°C) oven for 12 minutes until bottoms are lightly browned. Remove from baking sheet. Cool to room temperature. Makes 36 appetizers.

1 appetizer: 58 Calories; 3 g Total Fat; 101 mg Sodium; 3 g Protein; 4 g Carbohydrate; trace Dietary Fiber

Refried Bean Dip

Serve this warm with tortilla chips.

Can of refried beans	14 oz.	398 mL
Salsa	2 tsp.	10 mL
Lean ground beef	1 lb.	454 g
Salsa	1/2 cup	125 mL
Salt, to taste		
Grated medium Cheddar cheese	1 cup	250 mL
Salsa	1/2 cup	125 mL
Non-fat sour cream	1 cup	250 mL
Finely chopped green onion	2 tbsp.	30 mL
Shredded iceberg lettuce	1 cup	250 mL
Medium tomato, seeded and chopped	1	1

Combine beans and first amount of salsa in small bowl. Spread evenly in ungreased 10 inch (25 cm) pie plate.

Scramble-fry ground beef in non-stick frying pan until no longer pink. Drain.

Add second amount of salsa and salt. Cook for 5 minutes. Spread beef mixture evenly over bean mixture.

Sprinkle with cheese. Bake in 350°F (175°C) oven for 15 minutes until cheese is melted and beans are hot. Remove from oven. Cool for 10 minutes.

Spread with third amount of salsa.

Combine sour cream and green onion in small bowl. Spread over salsa.

Sprinkle with lettuce and tomato. Makes 4 cups (1 L).

2 tbsp. (30 mL): 56 Calories; 2.6 g Total Fat; 96 mg Sodium; 5 g Protein; 4 g Carbohydrate; trace Dietary Fiber

Pictured on page 18.

Appetizers

Roasted Pepper And Beef Triangles

These savory bites melt in your mouth. Make, bake and freeze ahead.
Best if reheated in the oven, not in the microwave.

Thinly sliced quartered onion	3 cups	750 mL
Hard margarine (or butter)	2 tbsp.	30 mL
Brown sugar, packed	2 tsp.	10 mL
Tenderloin steak, 3/4 - 1 inch (2 - 2.5 cm) thick, cut into 1/8 × 1 inch (0.3 × 2.5 cm) strips	8 oz.	225 g
Garlic clove, minced (or 1/4 tsp., 1 mL, powder)	1	1
Hard margarine (or butter)	1 tbsp.	15 mL
All-purpose flour	2 tbsp.	30 mL
Salt	1/2 tsp.	2 mL
Freshly ground pepper	1/4 tsp.	1 mL
Condensed beef broth	3/4 cup	175 mL
Chopped fresh sweet basil	1 tbsp.	15 mL
Grated Parmesan cheese	1/3 cup	75 mL
Part-skim ricotta cheese	8 oz.	250 g
Red Roasted Pepper, page 13, cut into slivers about 1 inch (2.5 cm) long	1	1
Frozen phyllo pastry sheets, thawed according to package directions	21	21

Sauté onion in first amount of margarine in non-stick frying pan for 10 minutes, stirring constantly. Reduce heat. Cook for 10 to 20 minutes, stirring frequently, until onion is browned and caramelized (not burned).

Add brown sugar. Stir. Transfer to small bowl.

Scramble-fry beef strips and garlic in second amount of margarine in same frying pan for 5 minutes.

Add flour, salt and pepper. Stir. Add broth. Heat and stir until boiling and thickened. Add onion mixture. Stir. Remove from heat. Cool.

Combine basil, both cheeses and red pepper in medium bowl. Add to beef mixture. Stir.

(continued on next page)

Lay 1 sheet of phyllo pastry on non-floured working surface. Spray lightly with cooking spray. Cover remainder with damp tea towel. Cut sheet crosswise into 4 equal strips. Fold each strip in half lengthwise. Place rounded teaspoonful beef mixture at 1 end. Fold 1 corner over to form triangle. Continue folding over triangles to end of strip. Be sure corners of triangle overlap to tightly enclose filling. Spray top of final triangle with cooking spray. Place other side on lightly greased baking sheet. Repeat with remaining sheets of phyllo and beef mixture. Bake in 400°F (205°C) oven for about 12 minutes until golden. Makes 84 triangles.

1 triangle: 28 Calories; 1.7 g Total Fat; 54 mg Sodium; 1 g Protein; 2 g Carbohydrate; trace Dietary Fiber

Beef-Stuffed Mushrooms

An exotic twist to stuffers—the filling can be made ahead and frozen.

Lean ground beef	1/4 lb.	113 g
Finely chopped pine nuts	2 tbsp.	30 mL
Finely chopped shallots (or green onion)	1/4 cup	60 mL
Fresh bread crumbs	1/4 cup	60 mL
Large egg, fork-beaten	1	1
Chopped sun-dried tomatoes, softened in boiling water for 10 minutes before chopping	3 tbsp.	50 mL
Chopped fresh sweet basil (or 1 1/2 tsp., 7 mL, dried)	2 tbsp.	30 mL
Salt	1/4 tsp.	1 mL
Lemon pepper	1/4 tsp.	1 mL
Medium whole fresh mushrooms, stems removed	16	16

Scramble-fry ground beef, pine nuts and shallots in small non-stick frying pan until beef is no longer pink and shallots are soft. Remove from heat.

Add bread crumbs, egg, tomato, basil, salt and lemon pepper. Mix well.

Stuff mushrooms with beef mixture, slightly mounding filling. Arrange in single layer on ungreased baking sheet. Bake in 400°F (205°C) oven for 10 minutes. Makes 16 stuffed mushrooms.

1 stuffed mushroom: 30 Calories; 1.6 g Total Fat; 34 mg Sodium; 2 g Protein; 2 g Carbohydrate; trace Dietary Fiber

Mexican Snackies

A nippy south-of-the-border appetizer with a biscuit crust.

Biscuit mix	2 cups	500 mL
Chopped fresh cilantro (or fresh parsley)	1/4 cup	60 mL
Water	1/2 cup	125 mL
Lean ground beef	1/2 lb.	225 g
Can of refried beans with green chilies	14 oz.	398 mL
Non-fat sour cream	1 cup	250 mL
Envelope of taco seasoning mix	1 1/4 oz.	35 g
Grated medium Cheddar cheese	1 1/2 cups	375 mL
Finely chopped green onion	1/2 cup	125 mL
Finely chopped green pepper	1/4 cup	60 mL
Finely chopped red pepper	1/4 cup	60 mL
Finely diced and seeded tomatoes	1 cup	250 mL
Finely chopped ripe pitted whole olives	1/4 cup	60 mL

Combine biscuit mix and cilantro in medium bowl. Add water. Stir until soft dough forms. Turn out onto surface lightly coated with biscuit mix. Knead about 10 times. Press into ungreased 15 x 10 x 1 inch (38 x 25 x 2.5 cm) jelly roll pan. (Dough will be very thin.) Bake in 400°F (205°C) oven for 10 minutes until golden and firm. Cool.

Scramble-fry ground beef in non-stick frying pan until no longer pink. Drain. Add refried beans. Mix. Cool slightly. Spread over crust.

Combine sour cream and seasoning mix in small bowl. Spread over beef mixture. Sprinkle with cheese.

Combine remaining 5 ingredients in medium bowl. Sprinkle over cheese. Pack down lightly. Chill for 1 hour. Cut into 1 1/2 x 2 inch (3.8 x 5 cm) pieces. Makes 40 appetizers.

1 appetizer: 79 Calories; 3.3 g Total Fat; 264 mg Sodium; 4 g Protein; 9 g Carbohydrate; trace Dietary Fiber

Pictured on page 18.

tip   *For juicier burgers, turn only once and do not flatten while barbecuing.*

Beefy Pepper Dim Sum

A nice combination of beef and pepper flavors.
The black bean sauce gives this dish a definite Asian flair.

Large green pepper	1	1
Large red pepper	1	1
Large yellow pepper	1	1
Lean ground beef	1/2 lb.	225 g
Garlic clove, minced (or 1/4 tsp., 1 mL, powder)	1	1
Salt	1/2 tsp.	2 mL
Chopped green onion	1/4 cup	60 mL
Finely diced water chestnuts	1/4 cup	60 mL
Black bean (or soy) sauce	1 1/2 tbsp.	25 mL
Large egg, fork-beaten	1	1
All-purpose flour	1 tbsp.	15 mL
Sesame seeds, toasted (see Tip, below)	1 tbsp.	15 mL

Cut all 3 peppers in half crosswise. Remove seeds and membranes. Cut each half into 4 pieces, for total of 24.

Scramble-fry ground beef, garlic and salt in non-stick frying pan for 4 minutes until beef is no longer pink but still moist. Remove from heat.

Add green onion, water chestnuts, black bean sauce, egg and flour. Mix well. Arrange pepper pieces, skin side down, on lightly greased baking sheet. Spoon beef mixture into pepper pieces.

Sprinkle with sesame seeds. Bake in 350°F (175°) oven for 15 minutes. Makes 24 appetizers.

1 appetizer: 26 Calories; 1.3 g Total Fat; 88 mg Sodium; 2 g Protein; 1 g Carbohydrate; trace Dietary Fiber

 To toast sesame seeds and nuts, place in single layer in ungreased shallow pan. Bake in 350°F (175°C) oven for 5 to 10 minutes, stirring or shaking often, until desired doneness.

Beef Souvlaki

A popular Greek dish. Serve this with rice and a Greek salad.

MARINADE		
Lemon juice	1/4 cup	60 mL
Olive (or cooking) oil	2 tbsp.	30 mL
Garlic cloves, minced (or 1/2 tsp., 2 mL, powder)	2	2
Chopped fresh rosemary leaves (or 3/4 tsp., 4 mL, dried)	1 tbsp.	15 mL
Dried whole oregano	1 tsp.	5 mL
Freshly ground pepper	1/4 tsp.	1 mL
Inside round (or outside round, sirloin tip or blade) steak, cut into 1 inch (2.5 cm) cubes	1 lb.	454 g
Metal skewers, 10 inch (25 cm) length	4	4
YOGURT SAUCE		
Salt	1/4 tsp.	1 mL
Peeled and grated English cucumber	1/2 cup	125 mL
Plain yogurt	1/2 cup	125 mL
Finely chopped fresh parsley (or 1 1/2 tsp., 7 mL, flakes)	2 tbsp.	30 mL
Garlic cloves, minced (or 1/2 tsp., 2 mL, powder)	2	2
Granulated sugar	1/2 tsp.	2 mL
Salt	1/2 tsp.	2 mL

Marinade: Combine first 6 ingredients in small bowl. Stir well.

Place beef cubes in shallow dish or resealable freezer bag. Pour marinade over beef. Stir or turn to coat. Cover or seal. Marinate in refrigerator for 4 hours or overnight, stirring or turning several times. Remove beef. Discard marinade.

Thread beef onto metal skewers, leaving small space between each piece. Barbecue skewers over medium heat for 10 to 15 minutes, turning often to brown evenly, until desired doneness.

Yogurt Sauce: Sprinkle first amount of salt over cucumber in small strainer. Drain for 15 minutes. Blot dry with paper towels.

Combine cucumber and remaining 5 ingredients in small bowl. Serve as dip. Serves 4.

1 serving: 179 Calories; 6.5 g Total Fat; 582 mg Sodium; 24 g Protein; 5 g Carbohydrate; trace Dietary Fiber

Barbecue

Barbecued Fajitas

Tender beef with a hint of lime.

MARINADE		
Lime juice	1/4 cup	60 mL
Olive (or cooking) oil	1 tbsp.	15 mL
Dried whole oregano	1 tbsp.	15 mL
Dried crushed chilies	1/2 tsp.	2 mL
Salt	1/4 tsp.	1 mL
Freshly ground pepper	1/8 tsp.	0.5 mL
Garlic cloves, minced (or 1/2 tsp., 2 mL, powder)	2	2
Flank steak	1 1/2 lbs.	680 g
Flour tortillas (10 inch, 25 cm, size)	8	8

TOPPINGS
Black Bean Salsa, page 14 (optional)
Chopped tomatoes (optional)
Shredded lettuce (optional)
Sliced avocados (optional)
Sliced hot peppers (optional)
Sliced green onions (optional)

Marinade: Combine first 7 ingredients in small bowl. Stir well.

Place steak in shallow dish or resealable freezer bag. Pour marinade over steak. Turn to coat. Cover or seal. Marinate in refrigerator overnight, turning several times. Remove steak. Discard marinade. Barbecue over medium heat for 5 to 7 minutes per side until desired doneness. Slice steak diagonally across grain into thin strips.

Wrap tortillas in foil. Heat over medium until warmed but still soft.

Toppings: Place 1/8 of beef strips down center of 1 tortilla, leaving 1/2 inch (12 mm) edge at bottom. Add selected toppings. Fold up bottom. Fold in sides, envelope-style, leaving top open. Repeat 7 more times with remaining beef tortillas and toppings. Makes 8 fajitas.

1 fajita: 265 Calories; 7.2 g Total Fat; 214 mg Sodium; 23 g Protein; 25 g Carbohydrate; trace Dietary Fiber

Teriyaki Burgers

A taste of Asia all wrapped up in a hamburger bun.

Reserved pineapple juice	1/4 cup	60 mL
Steak sauce	3 tbsp.	50 mL
Soy sauce	2 tbsp.	30 mL
Finely grated gingerroot (or 1/4 tsp., 1 mL, ground ginger)	1 1/2 tsp.	7 mL
Sesame seeds, toasted (see Tip, page 27)	1 1/2 tsp.	7 mL
Lean ground beef	1 lb.	454 g
Fresh bean sprouts, chopped	1 cup	250 mL
Green onions, thinly sliced	2	2
Can of pineapple slices, drained and juice reserved, blotted dry	8 oz.	227 mL
Hamburger buns, split	4	4

Combine first 5 ingredients in small bowl. Measure 1/4 cup (60 mL) sauce into medium bowl. Set aside remaining sauce.

Add ground beef, bean sprouts and green onion to sauce in medium bowl. Mix well. Shape into 4 patties. Barbecue over medium heat for 5 to 7 minutes per side, brushing often with remaining sauce, until no longer pink in center.

Barbecue pineapple slices for 2 to 3 minutes per side until heated through.

Serve burgers, topped with pineapple rings, in buns. Makes 4 burgers.

1 burger: 361 Calories; 12.8 g Total Fat; 987 mg Sodium; 26 g Protein; 36 g Carbohydrate; 1 g Dietary Fiber

Beer Burgers

Pass the burgers, pass the beer! Now a recipe that puts the two together.

Lean ground beef	2 lbs.	900 g
Beer	1/2 cup	125 mL
Large egg, fork-beaten	1	1
Dry bread crumbs	1/4 cup	60 mL
Dry onion soup mix (stir before measuring)	1 tbsp.	15 mL
Salt	1/2 tsp.	2 mL
Pepper	1/2 tsp.	2 mL

(continued on next page)

Barbecue

Medium onions, sliced	2	2
Hard margarine (or butter)	2 tbsp.	30 mL
Beer	1/2 cup	125 mL
Hamburger buns, split	8	8

Combine first 7 ingredients in large bowl. Mix well. Shape into 8 equal patties. Barbecue over medium-high heat for 5 minutes per side until no longer pink in center.

Sauté onion in margarine in small non-stick frying pan until soft. Add second amount of beer. Stir. Heat through.

Serve burgers, topped with onion mixture, in buns. Makes 8 burgers.

1 burger: 377 Calories; 15.8 g Total Fat; 690 mg Sodium; 26 g Protein; 29 g Carbohydrate; 1 g Dietary Fiber

Pictured on page 35 and back cover.

Green Pepper Burgers

Make twice as many burgers. Barbecue and freeze extras for a quick dinner.

Lean ground beef	1 1/2 lbs.	680 g
Soda cracker crumbs	3/4 cup	175 mL
Large egg	1	1
Skim evaporated milk	1/2 cup	125 mL
Very finely chopped onion	1/4 cup	60 mL
Very finely chopped green pepper	3/4 cup	175 mL
Dry mustard	1 1/2 tsp.	7 mL
Salt	1 1/2 tsp.	7 mL
Pepper	1/4 tsp.	1 mL
Canned pineapple slices, drained and blotted dry	6	6
Soy sauce	2 tbsp.	30 mL
Iceberg lettuce leaves	6	6
Kaiser rolls, cut in half	6	6

Combine first 9 ingredients in large bowl. Mix well. Shape into 6 patties. Barbecue over medium-low heat for 5 to 6 minutes per side until no longer pink in center.

Brush both sides of pineapple slices with soy sauce. Barbecue for 2 to 3 minutes per side until heated through.

Place lettuce leaf on bottom half of each bun. Top each with burger, pineapple slice and top half of bun. Serves 6.

1 serving: 436 Calories; 13.4 g Total Fat; 1530 mg Sodium; 30 g Protein; 47 g Carbohydrate; 2 g Dietary Fiber

Holiday Steak

A tasty treat for that special occasion. Serve with Pineapple Salsa, page 14.

Top sirloin (or strip loin or rib) steak, 3/4 - 1 inch (2 - 2.5 cm) thick	2 lbs.	900 g
Garlic clove, cut in half	1	1
MARINADE		
Steak sauce	2/3 cup	150 mL
Pineapple juice	1/2 cup	125 mL
Finely grated lime peel (about 1 medium)	1 tbsp.	15 mL
Freshly squeezed lime juice (about 1 medium)	1/4 cup	60 mL
Dried whole oregano	1/2 tsp.	2 mL
Ground cumin	1/2 tsp.	2 mL
Cayenne pepper	1/4 tsp.	1 mL

Rub both sides of steak with cut sides of garlic clove. Place steak in shallow dish or resealable freezer bag.

Marinade: Combine all 7 ingredients in small bowl. Stir well. Pour over steak. Turn to coat. Cover or seal. Marinate in refrigerator for 30 minutes, turning once. Remove steak, reserving marinade. Barbecue over medium-high heat for 5 to 7 minutes per side for medium, basting often with reserved marinade, until desired doneness. Bring any remaining marinade to a boil in small saucepan. Reduce heat. Simmer, uncovered, for 5 minutes. Serve over steak. Serves 6.

1 serving: 210 Calories; 5.9 g Total Fat; 65 mg Sodium; 31 g Protein; 7 g Carbohydrate; trace Dietary Fiber

Spanish Sirloin

Slice thin and serve either warm or cold with Aïoli Sauce, page 16.

Paprika	2 tbsp.	30 mL
Garlic cloves, minced (or 1 tsp., 5 mL, powder)	4	4
Lemon juice	2 tbsp.	30 mL
Freshly ground pepper	1 tsp.	5 mL

(continued on next page)

Barbecue

| Sirloin steak, 1 inch (2.5 cm) thick | 2 lbs. | 900 g |

Combine paprika, garlic, lemon juice and pepper in small bowl.

Spread paprika mixture on both sides of steak. Barbecue over medium heat for 8 to 10 minutes per side for medium until desired doneness. Let stand for 10 minutes. Slice steak thinly across grain. Serves 4.

1 serving: 281 Calories; 8.7 g Total Fat; 99 mg Sodium; 45 g Protein; 4 g Carbohydrate; 1 g Dietary Fiber

---

Taco Cheese Burgers

Nice for a change. These will make you think of Mexico. Make and freeze the single patties ahead of time. Fully defrost before adding the cheese and doubling up.

Lean ground beef	1 lb.	454 g
Dry bread crumbs	1/4 cup	60 mL
Large egg, fork-beaten	1	1
Small onion, finely chopped	1	1
Chili powder	1 tbsp.	15 mL
Dry mustard	1/2 tsp.	2 mL
Salt	1/2 tsp.	2 mL
Freshly ground pepper, to taste		
Thin slices of Monterey Jack cheese	4	4
Hamburger buns, split	4	4
Salsa (optional)		
Sour cream (optional)		

Combine first 8 ingredients in medium bowl. Mix well. Shape into 8 thin patties.

Place cheese slices on 4 patties. Top with remaining patties. Pinch edges to seal. Barbecue over medium-high heat for 6 to 8 minutes per side until beef is no longer pink inside.

Place buns, cut side down, on grill. Toast until lightly browned. Place patties on buns.

Top with salsa, sour cream and top halves of buns. Serves 4.

1 serving: 1841 Calories; 20 g Total Fat; 803 mg Sodium; 32 g Protein; 32 g Carbohydrate; 2 g Dietary Fiber

Pictured on page 35 and back cover.

Citrus Steaks

A quick dinner with a tangy sauce on tender beef.

Prepared orange juice	1/2 cup	125 mL
Ketchup	1/3 cup	75 mL
Lemon juice	1/4 cup	60 mL
Liquid honey	1/4 cup	60 mL
Dry mustard	2 tsp.	10 mL
Worcestershire sauce	1 tsp.	5 mL
Freshly grated orange peel	1 tsp.	5 mL
Paprika	1/2 tsp.	2 mL
Garlic clove, minced (or 1/4 tsp., 1 mL, powder)	1	1
Salt, to taste		
Pepper, to taste		
Rib-eye (or strip loin) steaks	4	4

Combine first 11 ingredients in small saucepan. Bring to a boil. Reduce heat. Simmer, uncovered, for 10 minutes until sauce is reduced to 3/4 cup (175 mL).

Barbecue steaks over medium heat for 2 minutes per side. Continue to barbecue for 4 to 5 minutes on each side for medium, brushing occasionally with sauce, until desired doneness. Bring remaining sauce to a boil in same saucepan. Reduce heat. Simmer, uncovered, for 5 minutes. Serve over steaks. Serves 4.

1 serving: 332 Calories; 9.7 g Total Fat; 342 mg Sodium; 33 g Protein; 29 g Carbohydrate; 1 g Dietary Fiber

1. Beer Burgers, page 30
2. Taco Cheese Burgers, page 33

Props Courtesy Of: The Bay

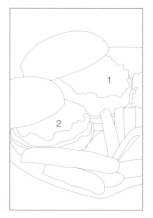

Salsa-Stuffed Steak

The hotter the salsa the hotter the surprise. Prepare in just ten minutes.

Sirloin (or strip loin or rib-eye) steak, 3/4 - 1 inch (2 - 2.5 cm) thick	1 1/2 lbs.	680 g
Salsa	1/2 cup	125 mL
Garlic cloves, minced (or 1/2 tsp., 2 mL, powder)	2	2
Small onion, finely chopped	1	1
Ground cumin (or dried whole oregano)	1 tsp.	5 mL
Pepper	1 tsp.	5 mL

Cut steak into 6 equal portions. Cut deep horizontal pocket into 1 side of each steak.

Combine salsa, garlic and onion in small bowl. Stuff salsa mixture into each pocket. Close opening with skewer. Sprinkle with cumin and pepper. Barbecue over medium-low heat for 5 to 7 minutes per side until desired doneness. Serves 4.

1 serving: 224 Calories; 6.4 g Total Fat; 118 mg Sodium; 35 g Protein; 6 g Carbohydrate; 1 g Dietary Fiber

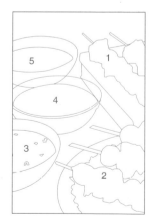

1. Thai Beef Kabobs, page 40
2. Hawaiian Kabobs, page 41
3. Golden Glaze, page 42
4. Teriyaki Marinade, page 43
5. Caribbean Marinade, page 42

Props Courtesy Of: Ikea

Peppercorn Roast

The Horseradish Sauce is very tasty and the perfect complement to this tender roast.

Inside round (or rump or sirloin tip) roast	3 1/2 lbs.	1.6 kg
Crushed whole peppercorns	2 tsp.	10 mL
Ground cloves	1/2 tsp.	2 mL
Dried whole oregano	1/2 tsp.	2 mL
Dijon mustard	2 tbsp.	30 mL
Lemon juice	1 tbsp.	15 mL
HORSERADISH SAUCE		
Sour cream	1 cup	250 mL
Grated fresh horseradish, drained	1 tbsp.	15 mL
Dijon mustard	1 tbsp.	15 mL
Lemon juice	1 tsp.	5 mL
Salt, to taste		
Pepper, to taste		

Place roast in large bowl.

Combine next 5 ingredients in small bowl. Rub over entire surface of roast. Cover. Chill overnight. Barbecue over medium heat, using indirect cooking method (page 10), for 35 minutes per lb. (75 minutes per kg) for rare or 45 minutes per lb. (100 minutes per kg) for medium.

Horseradish Sauce: Combine all 6 ingredients in small bowl. Mix well. Makes 1 cup (250 mL) sauce. Serve with roast. Serves 10.

1 serving: 223 Calories; 10.3 g Total Fat; 125 mg Sodium; 29 g Protein; 2 g Carbohydrate; trace Dietary Fiber

Tender And Tasty Beef Roast

Delicious barbecue flaror with a slight hint of wine and garlic.

Olive (or cooking) oil	3 tbsp.	50 mL
Dry red wine	1/2 cup	125 mL
Chili sauce	2 tbsp.	30 mL
Garlic clove, minced (or 1/4 tsp., 1 mL, powder)	1	1
Dry mustard	1/2 tsp.	2 mL
Lemon pepper	1/2 tsp.	2 mL
Boneless blade (or cross-rib) roast	3 1/2 lbs.	1.6 kg

(continued on next page)

Combine first 6 ingredients in small bowl.

Place roast in large bowl or resealable freezer bag. Pour marinade over roast. Turn to coat. Cover or seal. Marinate in refrigerator for at least 12 hours, turning several times. Remove roast, reserving marinade. Barbecue, over medium heat, using indirect cooking method (page 10), for 45 minutes per lb. (100 minutes per kg), brushing with marinade, until desired doneness. Meat thermometer should read 160°F (75°C) for medium. Discard any remaining marinade. Serves 10.

1 serving: 193 Calories; 11.2 g Total Fat; 90 mg Sodium; 19 g Protein; 1 g Carbohydrate; trace Dietary Fiber

---

Barbecued Beef Ribs

These spicy ribs will be a hit. Serve with baked potatoes.

Beef back ribs, cut into serving-size pieces	4 lbs.	1.8 kg
Water	3 tbsp.	50 mL
Freshly ground pepper, to taste		
BARBECUE SAUCE		
Chili sauce	1 cup	250 mL
Can of tomato sauce	7 1/2 oz.	213 mL
Garlic cloves, minced (or 1/2 tsp., 2 mL, powder)	2	2
Brown sugar, packed	1 tsp.	5 mL
Hot pepper sauce	1 tsp.	5 mL
Dijon mustard	2 tbsp.	30 mL
Lemon juice	1 tbsp.	15 mL
Dried crushed chilies	1 tsp.	5 mL

Divide ribs between 2 large sheets of heavy-duty foil (or double layers of regular foil). Sprinkle with water and pepper. Bring long sides of foil up over ribs and fold together. Crease to seal top. Press short sides of foil together at each end. Fold to seal each packet well. Barbecue packets over low heat for 1 1/2 hours, turning every 20 minutes.

Barbecue Sauce: Combine all 8 ingredients in medium saucepan. Bring to a boil. Reduce heat. Simmer, uncovered, for 10 to 15 minutes until slightly reduced and thickened. Remove ribs from foil. Place directly on grill over medium heat. Brush ribs well with sauce. Barbecue for 10 minutes, turning and basting once, until browned and glazed. Serves 6.

1 serving: 402 Calories; 20.1 g Total Fat; 932 mg Sodium; 39 g Protein; 16 g Carbohydrate; 3 g Dietary Fiber

Pictured on front cover.

Thai Beef Kabobs

In the true Thai tradition, these are spicy, savory, sweet and oh-so-good.

Top sirloin (or inside round) steak, 1 inch (2.5 cm) thick	1 lb.	454 g
PINEAPPLE PEANUT SAUCE		
Steak sauce	1/2 cup	125 mL
Reserved pineapple juice	1/2 cup	125 mL
Crunchy peanut butter	2 tbsp.	30 mL
Soy sauce	1 tbsp.	15 mL
Brown sugar, packed	1 tbsp.	15 mL
Dried crushed chilies	1 - 2 tsp.	5 - 10 mL
Curry powder	1/2 tsp.	2 mL
Garlic cloves, minced (or 1/2 tsp., 2 mL, powder)	2	2
Bamboo skewers, 10 inch (25 cm) length, soaked in water for 10 minutes	8	8
Can of pineapple chunks, drained and juice reserved	14 oz.	398 mL
Whole firm cantaloupe, cut into chunks	1	1
Large green pepper, cut into chunks	1	1

Cut steak into thin strips 1/4 inch (6 mm) thick and 5 inches (12.5 cm) long. Place in shallow dish or resealable freezer bag.

Pineapple Peanut Sauce: Combine first 8 ingredients in small bowl. Stir well. Pour over beef strips. Turn to coat. Cover or seal. Marinate in refrigerator for 30 minutes. Remove beef, reserving sauce.

Thread beef strips, accordion-style, onto skewers, alternating pineapple, cantaloupe and green pepper chunks between folds of beef. Barbecue over medium heat for 6 to 8 minutes, turning and brushing often with sauce until desired doneness. Bring remaining sauce to a boil in small saucepan. Reduce heat. Simmer, uncovered, for 5 minutes. Use as a dipping sauce for beef. Serves 4.

1 serving: 310 Calories; 9.2 g Total Fat; 370 mg Sodium; 28 g Protein; 31 g Carbohydrate; 3 g Dietary Fiber

Pictured on page 36.

Hawaiian Kabobs

A taste of the tropics. Serve these tender morsels on a bed of rice.

MARINADE

Reserved pineapple juice	1/2 cup	125 mL
Soy sauce	1 tbsp.	15 mL
Brown sugar, packed	1/4 cup	60 mL
White vinegar	1/4 cup	60 mL
Sirloin tip (or round) steak, cut into twelve 1 1/2 inch (3.8 cm) cubes	1 lb.	454 g
Water	3 tbsp.	50 mL
Cornstarch	1 tbsp.	15 mL
Can of pineapple chunks, drained and juice reserved	14 oz.	398 mL
Small green pepper, cut into 8 chunks	1	1
Large fresh mushrooms	8	8
Large cherry tomatoes	8	8
Metal skewers, 10 inch (25 cm) length	4	4

Marinade: Combine first 4 ingredients in small bowl. Stir well. Place beef cubes in shallow dish or resealable freezer bag. Pour marinade over beef. Stir or turn to coat. Cover or seal. Marinate in refrigerator for 6 to 8 hours or overnight, stirring or turning several times. Pour marinade into small saucepan.

Stir water into cornstarch in small cup until smooth. Gradually stir into marinade. Heat and stir until bubbling and thickened.

Alternate beef, pineapple, green pepper, mushrooms and tomato on skewers. Barbecue over medium-low heat for 6 to 8 minutes, turning and basting every 2 minutes with sauce, until desired doneness. Discard any remaining sauce. Makes 4 kabobs.

1 kabob: 278 Calories; 4.5 g Total Fat; 320 mg Sodium; 24 g Protein; 37 g Carbohydrate; 2 g Dietary Fiber

Pictured on page 36.

Paré Pointer
An autobiography is actually the life story of a favorite car.

Kabob Glazes and Marinades

Alternate cubes of beef and your favorite vegetables on skewers. Marinate beef in sauce ahead of time, if desired. Brush kabobs with marinade or glaze while barbecuing.

Caribbean Marinade

Wonderful lime and ginger flavor. Marinate beef for 4 hours or overnight.

Pineapple juice	1 cup	250 mL
Finely grated lime peel (about 1 medium)	1 tbsp.	15 mL
Freshly squeezed lime juice (about 1 medium)	1/4 cup	60 mL
Small onion, finely chopped	1	1
Garlic cloves, minced (or 1/2 tsp., 2 mL, powder)	2	2
Finely chopped gingerroot (or 1/4 tsp., 1 mL, ground ginger)	1 tsp.	5 mL
Hot pepper sauce	1/4 tsp.	1 mL

Combine all 7 ingredients in small bowl. Makes 1 1/2 cups (375 mL).

2 tbsp. (30 mL): 3 Calories; trace Total Fat; trace Sodium; trace Protein; 1 g Carbohydrate; trace Dietary Fiber

Pictured on page 36.

Golden Glaze

A sweet ginger-tasty glaze.

Beef bouillon powder	1 tbsp.	15 mL
Minced onion flakes	1 tbsp.	15 mL
Apricot jam	2/3 cup	150 mL
Water	1/2 cup	125 mL
Ground ginger	1/2 tsp.	2 mL

Combine all 5 ingredients in small saucepan. Bring to a boil. Reduce heat. Simmer, uncovered, for 5 minutes. Makes 1 cup (250 mL).

2 tbsp. (30 mL): 18 Calories; trace Total Fat; 54 mg Sodium; trace Protein; 5 g Carbohydrate; trace Dietary Fiber

Pictured on page 36.

Teriyaki Marinade

Nice tangy flavor. Marinate beef for four hours or overnight.

Soy sauce	1/4 cup	60 mL
Water	2 tbsp.	30 mL
Liquid honey	2 tbsp.	30 mL
Garlic clove, minced (or 1/4 tsp., 1 mL, powder)	1	1
Ground ginger	1/8 tsp.	0.5 mL

Combine all 5 ingredients in small saucepan. Bring to a boil. Reduce heat. Simmer, uncovered, for 5 minutes. Makes 1/2 cup (125 mL).

2 tbsp. (30 mL): 11 Calories; 0 g Total Fat; 251 mg Sodium; trace Protein; 3 g Carbohydrate; trace Dietary Fiber

Pictured on page 36.

Peppered Beef Skewers

Very tender and very peppery.

Olive (or cooking) oil	1 tbsp.	15 mL
Dijon mustard	1/2 tsp.	2 mL
Sirloin steak, cut into 1 inch (2.5 cm) cubes	1 lb.	454 g
Freshly ground pepper	2 tbsp.	30 mL
Bamboo skewers, 8 inch (20 cm) length, soaked in water for 10 minutes	6	6

Combine olive oil and mustard in small bowl. Stir well.

Brush mustard mixture onto beef cubes. Place pepper in shallow dish. Lightly roll beef in pepper. Push 6 beef cubes onto each skewer. Barbecue over medium heat for 8 to 10 minutes, turning once, until desired doneness. Makes 6 skewers.

1 skewer: 115 Calories; 5.1 g Total Fat; 40 mg Sodium; 15 g Protein; 1 g Carbohydrate; trace Dietary Fiber

Paré Pointer
When the ghost tried to frighten the banana, the banana split.

BBQ Party Salad

Invite guests early and have them cut and chop while you barbecue.
Great summer salad!

Dijon mustard	2 tbsp.	30 mL
Freshly ground pepper	1 tsp.	5 mL
Sirloin steak, 1 1/2 inch (3.8 cm) thick, blotted dry	2 lbs.	900 g
Ears of corn, husked	2	2
Olive (or cooking) oil	1 1/2 tbsp.	25 mL
Green, red or yellow Roasted Peppers, page 13, diced	3	3
Medium zucchini, with peel, sliced in half lengthwise	2	2
Red onions, sliced into 1/4 inch (6 mm) rings	2	2
Olive (or cooking) oil	1 1/2 tbsp.	25 mL
Tomatoes, diced	2	2
Sliced ripe pitted olives	1/2 cup	125 mL
DRESSING		
Balsamic (or red wine) vinegar	3 tbsp.	50 mL
Garlic cloves, minced (or 1/2 tsp., 2 mL, powder)	2	2
Salt	1 1/2 tsp.	7 mL
Pepper	1/2 tsp.	2 mL
Olive (or cooking) oil	1/3 cup	75 mL
Chopped fresh parsley (or 2 1/2 tsp., 12 mL, flakes)	3 tbsp.	50 mL
Chopped chives (or green onion)	3 tbsp.	50 mL
Chopped mixed salad greens	4 cups	1 L

Combine mustard and pepper in small bowl. Spread on both sides of steak. Barbecue over medium-high heat for 8 to 10 minutes per side until desired doneness. Cover with foil. Set aside.

Brush corn with some of first amount of olive oil. Barbecue over medium heat, turning until kernels start to crackle and are lightly golden. Cool slightly. Cut kernels off cob with sharp knife. Place in very large bowl. Add peppers.

(continued on next page)

Barbecue

Brush zucchini and onion rings with second amount of olive oil. Barbecue over medium heat until golden. Dice. Add to corn mixture. Stir.

Add tomato and olives.

Dressing: Combine vinegar, garlic, salt and pepper. Whisk in olive oil. Add parsley and chives. Toss with corn mixture. Remove steak from foil. Cut steak diagonally across grain into thin slices. Slice crosswise into 1 inch (2.5 cm) strips. Add to corn mixture. Toss.

Add salad greens. Toss to mix. Serves 8.

1 serving: 324 Calories; 19.6 g Total Fat; 444 mg Sodium; 25 g Protein; 14 g Carbohydrate; 3 g Dietary Fiber

Orange-Glazed BBQ Ribs

First you'll notice the taste of orange, followed by a hint of soy sauce. Simply wonderful.

Burgundy wine	3/4 cup	175 mL
Cooking oil	1/2 cup	125 mL
Orange marmalade	3/4 cup	175 mL
Soy sauce	1/4 cup	60 mL
Garlic clove, minced (or 1/4 tsp., 1 mL, powder)	1	1
Finely grated gingerroot (or 1 1/2 tsp., 7 mL, ground ginger)	2 tbsp.	30 mL
Dry mustard	2 tsp.	10 mL
Salt	1 tsp.	5 mL
Pepper	1/2 tsp.	2 mL
Beef ribs (about 4 lbs., 1.8 kg), individually cut	12	12

Combine first 9 ingredients in small bowl.

Place ribs in shallow dish or resealable freezer bag. Pour marinade over ribs. Turn to coat. Cover or seal. Marinate in refrigerator overnight, turning several times. Remove ribs, reserving marinade. Barbecue over medium-low heat for 30 to 40 minutes, turning and brushing frequently with reserved marinade, until tender. Discard any remaining marinade. Serves 6.

1 serving: 420 Calories; 25.3 g Total Fat; 666 mg Sodium; 30 g Protein; 15 g Carbohydrate; 2 g Dietary Fiber

Taco-On-A-Platter

This colorful platter is sure to please with a nice blend of chili and cumin.

MEAT SAUCE

Lean ground beef	2 lbs.	900 g
Medium onion, chopped	1	1
Cans of tomato paste (5 1/2 oz., 156 mL, each)	2	2
Can of crushed tomatoes	14 oz.	398 mL
Chili powder	2 tbsp.	30 mL
Ground cumin	1 tsp.	5 mL
Garlic powder	1/2 tsp.	2 mL
Salt	2 tsp.	10 mL
Can of beans in tomato sauce, with liquid	28 oz.	796 mL
Corn chips, broken	2 cups	500 mL
Hot cooked long grain white rice	2 cups	500 mL
Grated medium Cheddar cheese	2 cups	500 mL
Medium red onion, chopped	1	1
Head of iceberg lettuce, shredded	1	1
Medium tomatoes, chopped	3	3
Sliced ripe pitted olives	1/3 cup	75 mL

Picante sauce (or salsa), optional

Meat Sauce: Scramble-fry ground beef and first amount of onion in large non-stick frying pan. Drain.

Add next 6 ingredients. Mix well. Simmer, uncovered, for 15 minutes.

Add beans. Stir to heat through.

Layer next 7 ingredients in order given on large platter.

Serve with picante sauce. Serves 12.

1 serving: *429 Calories; 17.7 g Total Fat; 1032 mg Sodium; 26 g Protein; 44 g Carbohydrate; 10 g Dietary Fiber*

Paré Pointer
Even computers in restaurants have a byte now and then.

Creamy Greek Bake

A simpler, quicker version of the traditional Greek pastitsio casserole.

Light salad dressing (or mayonnaise)	1/2 cup	125 mL
All-purpose flour	1/4 cup	60 mL
Milk	2 cups	500 mL
Salt	1/2 tsp.	2 mL
Lean ground beef	1 lb.	454 g
Chopped onion	1 cup	250 mL
Garlic clove, minced (or 1/4 tsp., 1 mL, powder)	1	1
Can of tomato paste	5 1/2 oz.	156 mL
Ground cinnamon	1/4 tsp.	1 mL
Large egg, fork-beaten	1	1
Ground nutmeg	1/4 tsp.	1 mL
Grated Parmesan cheese	1/2 cup	125 mL
Elbow macaroni, cooked and drained (about 3/4 cup, 175 mL, uncooked)	1 1/2 cups	375 mL
Paprika	1/8 tsp.	0.5 mL

Stir salad dressing into flour in medium saucepan until smooth.

Gradually stir in milk. Add salt. Stir as you bring to a boil. Remove from heat. Pour into medium bowl. Let cool.

Scramble-fry ground beef, onion and garlic in non-stick frying pan until beef is no longer pink and onion is soft. Drain.

Add tomato paste and cinnamon. Stir. Remove from heat.

Add egg, nutmeg and cheese to milk mixture. Mix well. Add macaroni. Stir. Layer macaroni mixture in three parts alternating with beef mixture in two parts, beginning and ending with macaroni mixture in lightly greased 3 quart (3 L) casserole. Sprinkle with paprika. Cover. Bake in 350°F (175°) oven for 20 to 25 minutes until hot and set. Serves 6.

1 serving: 371 Calories; 16.6 g Total Fat; 652 mg Sodium; 25 g Protein; 30 g Carbohydrate; 3 g Dietary Fiber

Jambalaya Casserole

A good combination of ingredients that go well together for a satisfying taste.

Lean ground beef	1 lb.	454 g
Garlic clove, minced (or 1/4 tsp., 1 mL, powder)	1	1
Medium onion, chopped	1	1
Medium green pepper, chopped	1	1
Chopped fresh parsley (or 3/4 tsp., 4 mL, flakes)	1 tbsp.	15 mL
Worcestershire sauce	1/2 tsp.	2 mL
Chili powder	1/2 tsp.	2 mL
Salt	1 tsp.	5 mL
Pepper	1/4 tsp.	1 mL
Can of stewed tomatoes, with juice, chopped	28 oz.	796 mL
Long grain white rice, uncooked	3/4 cup	175 mL
Bay leaf	1	1
Paprika	1 tsp.	5 mL

Scramble-fry ground beef, garlic and onion in non-stick frying pan until beef is no longer pink. Drain.

Combine remaining 10 ingredients in large bowl. Add beef mixture. Mix well. Turn into lightly greased 3 quart (3 L) casserole. Cover. Bake in 350°F (175°C) oven for 1 1/4 hours until rice is cooked. Serves 6.

1 serving: 249 Calories; 6.8 g Total Fat; 853 mg Sodium; 17 g Protein; 31 g Carbohydrate; 3 g Dietary Fiber

Fast Fixin' Nacho Casserole

This dish can be mild or spicy depending on the type of salsa used.

Coarsely chopped cooked lean beef	1 1/4 cups	300 mL
Salsa	3/4 cup	175 mL
Grated Monterey Jack cheese	1/3 cup	75 mL
Grated Monterey Jack cheese	2/3 cup	150 mL
Corn tortilla chips (optional)		

(continued on next page)

Combine beef, salsa and first amount of cheese in medium bowl. Turn into lightly greased 1 quart (1 L) casserole. Cover. Bake in 350°F (175°C) oven for 20 minutes.

Top with second amount of cheese. Bake, uncovered, in 350°F (175°C) oven for 10 minutes until cheese is melted.

Serve with tortilla chips. Serves 4.

1 serving: 269 Calories; 14.8 g Total Fat; 216 mg Sodium; 21 g Protein; 13 g Carbohydrate; 1 g Dietary Fiber

Sloppy Joe Pasta Casserole

Zesty with a slightly sweet taste.
Nice traditional Sloppy Joe flavor combined with pasta.

Ziti (or penne) pasta, uncooked	2 cups	500 mL
Lean ground beef	1 1/2 lbs.	680 g
Diced onion	1 cup	250 mL
Diced green pepper	1 cup	250 mL
Prepared mustard	1 tbsp.	15 mL
Brown sugar, packed	1/4 cup	60 mL
Apple cider vinegar	2 tbsp.	30 mL
Worcestershire sauce	2 tbsp.	30 mL
Can of stewed tomatoes, with juice	28 oz.	796 mL
Can of tomato sauce	7 1/2 oz.	213 mL
Can of tomato paste	5 1/2 oz.	156 mL
Ground allspice	1/2 tsp.	2 mL
Hot pepper sauce	1/2 tsp.	2 mL
Dried whole oregano	1/2 tsp.	2 mL
Salt	1 tsp.	5 mL
Pepper	1/4 tsp.	1 mL

Cook pasta according to package directions. Drain. Keep in cold water.

Scramble-fry ground beef in non-stick frying pan for 5 minutes. Add onion and green pepper. Sauté until beef is no longer pink and onion is soft. Drain.

Add remaining 12 ingredients. Mix well. Bring to a boil. Reduce heat. Cover. Simmer for 20 minutes. Add drained pasta. Stir. Spoon into lightly greased 9 × 13 inch (22 × 33 cm) pan or 3 quart (3 L) casserole. Bake, uncovered, in 350°F (175°C) oven for 20 minutes until hot. Serves 8.

1 serving: 330 Calories; 8 g Total Fat; 858 mg Sodium; 22 g Protein; 44 g Carbohydrate; 4 g Dietary Fiber

Spicy Italian Casserole

Tender beef in a delicious tomato sauce.

Rotini (or fusilli) pasta, uncooked	3/4 cup	175 mL
Sirloin steak, cut into 2 1/2 × 1/4 inch (6.4 × 0.6 cm) strips (or 2 cups, 500 mL, cubed cooked beef)	1 lb.	454 g
Cooking oil	1 tsp.	5 mL
Small onion, chopped	1	1
Chopped green pepper	1/2 cup	125 mL
Can of stewed tomatoes, with juice, chopped	19 oz.	540 mL
Can of tomato sauce	7 1/2 oz.	213 mL
All-purpose flour	3 tbsp.	50 mL
Beef bouillon powder	2 tsp.	10 mL
Dried whole oregano	1/2 tsp.	2 mL
Salt	1/4 tsp.	1 mL
Pepper, to taste		
Grated part-skim mozzarella cheese, for garnish		

Cook pasta according to package directions. Drain. Keep in cold water.

Sauté beef strips in cooking oil in frying pan for 5 minutes. Add onion and green pepper. Sauté until onion is slightly soft. Add tomatoes. Stir.

Combine tomato sauce and flour in small bowl. Mix well.

Add tomato sauce mixture, bouillon powder, oregano, salt and pepper to beef mixture. Heat and stir until boiling and thickened. Spoon into ungreased 1 1/2 quart (1.5 L) casserole. Add drained pasta. Stir. Bake, uncovered, in 350°F (175°C) oven for 30 minutes until hot.

Garnish individual servings with mozzarella cheese. Serves 4.

1 serving: 296 Calories; 6.1 g Total Fat; 1139 mg Sodium; 28 g Protein; 33 g Carbohydrate; 3 g Dietary Fiber

Pictured on page 53.

tip *Sear beef cubes the day before and store in the refrigerator (or freeze for future use), then complete the recipe the next day.*

Company Chili

A traditional full-bodied chili with a bit of zip. A good make-ahead. Freezes well.

Chuck steak (or stewing beef), trimmed of all visible fat, sinew removed and beef cut into 3/4 inch (2 cm) cubes	2 1/2 lbs.	1.1 kg
Cooking oil	1 tsp.	5 mL
Large onion, chopped	1	1
Celery ribs, chopped	3	3
Large green pepper, chopped	1	1
Garlic cloves, minced (or 1/2 tsp., 2 mL, powder)	2	2
Jalapeño peppers, seeded and diced (see Note)	2	2
Can of diced tomatoes, with juice	28 oz.	796 mL
Can of tomato paste	5 1/2 oz.	156 mL
Water	1 cup	250 mL
Chili powder	1 1/2 tbsp.	25 mL
Brown sugar, packed	1 tbsp.	15 mL
Salt	1 tsp.	5 mL
Pepper	1/8 tsp.	0.5 mL
Worcestershire sauce	1 tsp.	5 mL
White vinegar	1 tbsp.	15 mL
Cans of kidney beans (14 oz., 398 mL, each), drained and rinsed	2	2

Grated medium Cheddar cheese, for garnish
Diced red onion, for garnish

Sear beef cubes in cooking oil in ovenproof Dutch oven on medium-high until browned on all sides. Reduce heat to medium.

Add next 5 ingredients. Stir. Cook for 10 minutes until vegetables are soft.

Add next 10 ingredients. Mix well. Bring to a simmer. Cover. Bake in 325°F (160°C) oven for 1 hour until beef is tender. Remove lid. Bake for 30 minutes.

Garnish individual servings with cheese and onion. Serves 8.

1 serving: 304 Calories; 6.4 g Total Fat; 948 mg Sodium; 33 g Protein; 30 g Carbohydrate; 10 g Dietary Fiber

Pictured on page 53.

Note: Wear gloves when chopping jalapeño peppers and avoid touching your eyes.

Chunky Chili

A lovely tomato flavor with just the right amount of green pepper.

Top round (or sirloin tip) steak, cut into 3/4 inch (2 cm) cubes	1 lb.	454 g
Medium onion, chopped	1	1
Cooking oil	1 tsp.	5 mL
Cans of Mexican-style stewed tomatoes (14 oz., 398 mL, each), with juice (see Note)	2	2
Can of kidney beans, with liquid	14 oz.	398 mL
Medium green pepper, chopped	1	1
Long grain white rice, uncooked	3/4 cup	175 mL
Water	1 cup	250 mL
Cocoa	1 tbsp.	15 mL
Chili powder	2 tsp.	10 mL
Salt	1/2 tsp.	2 mL

Sear beef cubes and onion in cooking oil in large non-stick frying pan on medium-high until beef is browned.

Add remaining 8 ingredients. Stir. Bring to a boil. Reduce heat. Cover. Simmer for 1 hour until beef and rice are tender. Serves 6.

1 serving: 289 Calories; 4.4 g Total Fat; 810 mg Sodium; 22 g Protein; 42 g Carbohydrate; 7 g Dietary Fiber

Note: If Mexican or chili-style stewed tomatoes are not available, use regular stewed tomatoes plus an additional 2 tsp. (10 mL) chili powder.

1. Spicy Italian Casserole, page 50
2. Company Chili, page 51

Props Courtesy Of: Chintz & Company
Libicz's Kitchen Essentials

Skillet Chili 'N' Pasta

Only a frying pan is needed to
prepare this easy one-dish meal.

Lean ground beef	3/4 lb.	340 g
Medium onion, diced	1	1
Garlic clove, minced (or 1/4 tsp., 1 mL, powder)	1	1
Can of stewed tomatoes, with juice, chopped	28 oz.	796 mL
Tomato juice	1 cup	250 mL
Can of kidney beans, with liquid	14 oz.	398 mL
Chili powder	1 tbsp.	15 mL
Fusilli pasta, uncooked	1 cup	250 mL
Chopped fresh sweet basil (or 1 1/2 tsp., 7 mL, dried)	2 tbsp.	30 mL

Scramble-fry ground beef, onion and garlic in non-stick frying pan until beef is no longer pink and onion is soft. Drain.

Add next 4 ingredients. Stir. Bring to a boil.

Add pasta and basil. Stir. Bring to a boil. Reduce heat. Cover. Simmer for 15 minutes until pasta is tender. Serves 4.

1 serving: 383 Calories; 8.4 g Total Fat; 1198 mg Sodium; 27 g Protein; 53 g Carbohydrate; 11 g Dietary Fiber

1. Beef And Greens Stir-Fry, page 148
2. Indian-Spiced Beef, page 145
3. Pineapple Beef Stir-Fry, page 147

Props Courtesy Of: Le Gnome

Tamale Pie

Just enough spice. The tomatoes add a nice flavor.

Lean ground beef	1 1/2 lbs.	680 g
Garlic cloves, minced (or 1/2 tsp., 2 mL, powder)	2	2
Can of stewed tomatoes, with juice, chopped	28 oz.	796 mL
Chili powder	2 tsp.	10 mL
Salt	1/8 tsp.	0.5 mL
Freshly ground pepper	1/8 tsp.	0.5 mL
Chopped fresh parsley (or 3 tsp., 15 mL, flakes)	1/4 cup	60 mL
All-purpose flour	1 cup	250 mL
Cornmeal	3/4 cup	175 mL
Granulated sugar	1 tbsp.	15 mL
Baking powder	2 tsp.	10 mL
Baking soda	1/2 tsp.	2 mL
Salt	1/2 tsp.	2 mL
Grated Parmesan cheese	3 tbsp.	50 mL
Large egg	1	1
Buttermilk (or sour milk, see Note)	1 cup	250 mL
Cooking oil	1/4 cup	60 mL
Dashes of hot pepper sauce	3	3

Scramble-fry ground beef and garlic in large non-stick frying pan until beef is no longer pink. Drain.

Add tomatoes and chili powder. Bring to a boil. Reduce heat. Simmer, uncovered, until mixture is consistency of thick spaghetti sauce.

Add salt, pepper and parsley. Stir. Turn into ungreased deep 10 inch (25 cm) pie plate.

Combine flour, cornmeal, sugar, baking powder, baking soda and salt in large bowl. Mix well. Add cheese. Toss lightly.

Beat remaining 4 ingredients together in medium bowl. Add to cornmeal mixture. Stir until just moistened. Spread evenly over beef mixture. Bake in 375°F (190°C) oven for 30 minutes until topping is golden. Wooden pick inserted in center should come out clean. Serves 6.

(continued on next page)

Note: To make sour milk, add milk to 1 tbsp. (15 mL) white vinegar or
lemon juice in 1 cup (250 mL) measuring cup. Stir.

Spaghetti Pie

Excellent sun-dried tomato and garlic flavor.

Spaghetti, uncooked	8 oz.	225 g
Dried sweet basil, crushed	1 tsp.	5 mL
Lean ground beef	1 lb.	454 g
Can of tomato sauce	14 oz.	398 mL
Garlic clove, minced (or 1/4 tsp., 1 mL, powder)	1	1
Dried whole oregano	1 tsp.	5 mL
Chopped sun-dried tomatoes, softened in boiling water for 10 minutes before chopping	1/4 cup	60 mL
Can of marinated artichoke hearts, drained and rinsed	6 oz.	170 g
Grated part-skim mozzarella cheese	1 cup	250 mL

Cook spaghetti according to package directions. Drain well. Turn into
large bowl.

Add basil. Toss. Turn into lightly greased 2 1/2 quart (2.5 L) casserole or
deep 10 inch (25 cm) pie plate. Press firmly against bottom and up sides
to form thick crust.

Scramble-fry ground beef in non-stick frying pan until beef is no longer
pink. Drain.

Add tomato sauce, garlic, oregano and tomatoes. Stir. Cover. Simmer for
6 minutes, stirring occasionally. Pour beef mixture into spaghetti crust.

Arrange artichoke hearts on top of beef mixture. Bake, uncovered, in 350°F
(175°C) oven for 15 to 20 minutes until set.

Sprinkle with cheese. Bake for 5 minutes until cheese is melted. Cuts into
6 wedges.

Beef And Rice Quiche

A beautiful quiche with just the right amount of everything.

Warm cooked long grain white rice	2 cups	500 mL
Chopped chives	2 tbsp.	30 mL
Large egg	1	1
Large eggs, fork-beaten	3	3
Can of skim evaporated milk	13 1/2 oz.	385 mL
Sliced green onion	1/2 cup	125 mL
Chopped fresh parsley (or 3/4 tsp., 4 mL, flakes)	1 tbsp.	15 mL
Liquid smoke	1/2 tsp.	2 mL
Salt	1/2 tsp.	2 mL
Dry mustard	1/2 tsp.	2 mL
Finely chopped cooked lean beef	1 cup	250 mL
Grated medium Cheddar cheese	1 cup	250 mL
Red Roasted Pepper, page 13, cut into 8 strips	1	1

Combine rice, chives and first egg in small bowl. Turn into lightly greased deep 10 inch (25 cm) pie plate. Press firmly against bottom and up sides to form crust. Press with rubber spatula to ensure there are no holes. Bake in 350°F (175°C) oven for 5 minutes.

Combine next 9 ingredients in large bowl. Mix well. Gently pour into rice shell.

Arrange red pepper in pinwheel design over top. Bake, uncovered, in 350°F (175°C) oven for 45 minutes until center is set. Immediately run knife around edge to loosen crust. Let stand for 10 minutes before cutting. Cuts into 8 wedges.

1 wedge: 245 Calories; 8.8 g Total Fat; 368 mg Sodium; 18 g Protein; 23 g Carbohydrate; trace Dietary Fiber

Traditional Lasagne

Great Italian flavor to this popular dish.

Lasagna noodles	12	12
Lean ground beef	1 lb.	454 g
Garlic clove, minced (or 1/4 tsp., 1 mL, powder)	1	1
Chopped onion	1 cup	250 mL

(continued on next page)

Dried whole oregano	1 tsp.	5 mL
Pepper	1/2 tsp.	2 mL
Can of stewed tomatoes, with juice, chopped	14 oz.	398 mL
Can of tomato paste	5 1/2 oz.	156 mL
Can of tomato sauce	7 1/2 oz.	213 mL
Dry curd cottage cheese	1 1/2 cups	375 mL
Grated part-skim mozzarella cheese	1 cup	250 mL
Grated Parmesan cheese	1/4 cup	60 mL
Garlic clove, minced (or 1/4 tsp., 1 mL, powder)	1	1
Parsley flakes	1 tbsp.	15 mL
Dried sweet basil	2 tsp.	10 mL
Salt	1/2 tsp.	2 mL
Grated part-skim mozzarella cheese	2 cups	500 mL
Grated Parmesan cheese	1/4 cup	60 mL

Cook lasagna noodles according to package directions. Drain. Keep in cold water.

Scramble-fry ground beef, first amount of garlic and onion in non-stick frying pan until beef is no longer pink and onion is soft. Drain.

Add oregano and pepper. Stir. Add tomatoes, tomato paste and tomato sauce. Stir. Simmer, uncovered, for 10 minutes.

Combine next 7 ingredients in large bowl.

To assemble, layer in lightly greased 9 x 13 inch (22 x 33 cm) pan as follows:

1. 1 cup (250 mL) meat sauce
2. Layer of 4 noodles
3. 1/2 of remaining meat sauce
4. Layer of 4 noodles
5. All of cottage cheese mixture
6. Layer of 4 noodles
7. Remaining meat sauce
8. All of mozzarella and Parmesan cheese

Cover with lightly greased foil. Bake in 350°F (175°C) oven for 30 minutes. Remove foil. Bake for 15 minutes until cheese is lightly browned. Let stand for 10 minutes before cutting. To make ahead and chill, allow extra 30 minutes baking time. Serves 8.

1 serving: 423 Calories; 14.9 g Total Fat; 794 mg Sodium; 35 g Protein; 37 g Carbohydrate; 3 g Dietary Fiber

Mexican Lasagne

A little on the spicy side. Excellent flavor.

Lean ground beef	1 lb.	454 g
Medium onion, chopped	1	1
Garlic clove, minced (or 1/4 tsp., 1 mL, powder)	1	1
Chopped fresh cilantro (or fresh parsley)	1/4 cup	60 mL
Salsa	3 cups	750 mL
Chili powder	1 tsp.	5 mL
Can of tomato sauce	7 1/2 oz.	213 mL
Water	1 cup	250 mL
Part-skim ricotta cheese	16 oz.	500 g
Large egg	1	1
Salt	1/2 tsp.	2 mL
Pepper	1/4 tsp.	1 mL
Lasagna noodles, uncooked	12	12
Grated Monterey Jack cheese	2 1/2 cups	625 mL

Scramble-fry ground beef in large non-stick frying pan for 5 minutes.

Add onion, garlic and cilantro. Cook until beef is no longer pink and onion is soft. Drain.

Add salsa, chili powder, tomato sauce and water. Heat and stir until boiling. Remove from heat.

Combine ricotta cheese, egg, salt and pepper in medium bowl.

To assemble, layer in lightly greased 9 x 13 inch (22 x 33 cm) pan as follows:

1. 1 1/4 cups (300 mL) meat sauce
2. Layer of 4 noodles
3. 1 1/4 cups (300 mL) meat sauce
4. Layer of 4 noodles
5. All of ricotta cheese mixture
6. Layer of 4 noodles
7. Remaining meat sauce
8. All of Monterey Jack cheese

Cover pan tightly with lightly greased foil. Bake in 350°F (175°C) oven for 1 1/4 hours. Remove foil. Bake for 15 minutes until cheese is golden. Let stand for 10 minutes before cutting. Serves 8.

1 serving: 479 Calories; 22.3 g Total Fat; 684 mg Sodium; 33 g Protein; 37 g Carbohydrate; 3 g Dietary Fiber

Penne With Wine Vegetable Sauce

This complete meal has a gentle blend of peppers, fresh basil, tomato and wine.

Penne pasta, uncooked	8 oz.	225 g
Hard margarine (or butter)	2 tbsp.	30 mL
All-purpose flour	3 tbsp.	50 mL
Skim evaporated milk	1 cup	250 mL
Lean ground beef	1 lb.	454 g
Large onion, cut into lengthwise slivers	1	1
Garlic cloves, minced (or 1 tsp., 5 mL, powder)	4	4
Sliced fresh mushrooms	3 cups	750 mL
Medium red pepper, cut into 2 inch (5 cm) strips	1	1
Dry white (or alcohol-free) wine	1 cup	250 mL
Can of tomatoes, with juice, chopped	28 oz.	796 mL
Finely chopped fresh sweet basil (or 3 tsp., 15 mL, dried)	1/4 cup	60 mL
Freshly ground pepper, for garnish		
Grated Parmesan cheese, for garnish		

Cook pasta according to package directions. Drain. Keep in cold water.

Melt margarine in small saucepan. Stir in flour until smooth. Gradually stir in evaporated milk. Heat and stir until sauce is smooth and bubbling. Remove from heat. Cover. Set aside.

Scramble-fry ground beef in large saucepan until no longer pink. Drain.

Add onion and garlic. Sauté until onion is soft.

Add mushrooms and red pepper. Cook for 5 minutes until vegetables release their juices and mixture is bubbling.

Add wine and tomatoes with juice. Bring to a boil. Stir in milk mixture and basil. Add pasta. Stir.

Garnish with pepper and Parmesan cheese. Serves 6.

1 serving: *435 Calories; 11.5 g Total Fat; 354 mg Sodium; 25 g Protein; 51 g Carbohydrate; 3 g Dietary Fiber*

Pictured on page 71.

Sesame Kabobs With Spinach

Tender and flavorful chunks of beef and peppers laid over a bed of spinach.
Serve with rice for a full meal.

Soy sauce	1/3 cup	75 mL
Sesame oil	1/3 cup	75 mL
Sesame seeds	2 tbsp.	30 mL
Freshly grated gingerroot (or 1 1/2 tsp., 7 mL, ground ginger)	2 tbsp.	30 mL
Top inside round (or sirloin tip) steak, cut into 1 inch (2.5 cm) cubes	1 lb.	454 g
Large red onion, cut into 8 wedges	1	1
Large yellow pepper, cut into 1 inch (2.5 cm) chunks	1	1
Large orange pepper, cut into 1 inch (2.5 cm) chunks	1	1
Bamboo skewers, 10 inch (25 cm) length, soaked in water for 10 minutes	8	8
Fresh spinach	10 oz.	285 g
Large tomato, cut into wedges	1	1
Reserved marinade		

Combine first 4 ingredients in medium bowl. Reserve 1/4 cup (60 mL).

Place beef cubes in shallow dish or reseablabe freezer bag. Pour remaining marinade over beef. Stir or turn to coat. Cover or seal. Marinate in refrigerator for 2 hours. Remove beef, reserving marinade.

Alternate beef, onion, yellow pepper and orange pepper on each skewer. Baste with marinade. Discard any remaining marinade. Place skewers on broiler pan rack.

Combine spinach, tomato and reserved marinade in bottom of broiler pan. Place rack of skewers on top of pan. Broil 7 to 9 inches (18 to 22 cm) from heat for 12 to 15 minutes for medium-rare, turning once. Drain spinach and tomato. Place on warmed platter. Lay kabobs on spinach mixture. Serve immediately. Makes 8 kabobs with 2 cups (500 mL) spinach mixture.

1 kabob plus 1/4 cup (60 mL) spinach mixture: 128 Calories; 6.3 g Total Fat; 325 mg Sodium; 13 g Protein; 5 g Carbohydrate; 2 g Dietary Fiber

Pictured on front cover.

Swiss Steak And Peppers

For a milder flavor, remove the seeds and membrane from the jalapeño pepper.

Minute steak, cut into serving-size pieces	1 1/2 lbs.	680 g
Cooking oil	1 tsp.	5 mL
Dried thyme	1/2 tsp.	2 mL
Salt	3/4 tsp.	4 mL
Pepper	1/4 tsp.	1 mL
Medium onion, chopped	1	1
Jalapeño pepper, with seeds and membrane, cut into 1/8 inch (3 mm) slices (see Note)	1	1
Water	1/4 cup	60 mL
Medium tomatoes, chopped	4	4
Small green pepper, cut into 1 inch (2.5 cm) chunks	1	1
Small yellow pepper, cut into 1 inch (2.5 cm) chunks	1	1

Sear beef on both sides in cooking oil in large frying pan on medium-high.

Sprinkle with thyme, salt and pepper. Top with onion and jalapeño pepper. Add water. Cover. Reduce heat. Simmer for 45 minutes.

Add tomato and both peppers. Cover. Simmer for 30 minutes. Remove beef and vegetables with slotted spoon to warmed platter. Heat remaining liquid, uncovered, for 8 to 10 minutes, stirring frequently, until reduced and slightly thickened. Return beef and vegetables to sauce mixture. Heat through. Serves 6.

1 serving: 168 Calories; 5.2 g Total Fat; 408 mg Sodium; 23 g Protein; 6 g Carbohydrate; 1 g Dietary Fiber

Note: Wear gloves when chopping jalapeño peppers and avoid touching your eyes.

 Never allow raw beef to come in contact with cooked beef or any other edible food item.

Company Rouladen

A variation of a famous German dish. Wonderful blend of flavors.

Bacon slices, cooked almost crisp, drained and cut into 1/2 inch (12 mm) pieces	8	8
Jar of marinated mushrooms, drained and chopped	8 oz.	227 mL
Rouladen steaks, 1/4 inch (6 mm) thick (about 1 1/2 lbs., 680 g, total)	8	8
All-purpose flour	1/4 cup	60 mL
Seasoned salt	1 tsp.	5 mL
Pepper	1/4 tsp.	1 mL
Water	3/4 cup	175 mL
Can of condensed beef consommé	10 oz.	284 mL
Chopped onion	1/2 cup	125 mL
Garlic clove, minced (or 1/4 tsp., 1 mL, powder)	1	1
Bay leaf	1	1
Water	1/4 cup	60 mL
All-purpose flour	3 tbsp.	50 mL

Combine bacon and mushrooms in small bowl. Place equal amounts of mushroom mixture on each of 8 steaks. Roll up, tucking in ends as you roll. Tie with butcher's string or secure with wooden picks.

Combine first amount of flour, seasoned salt and pepper in small plastic bag. Add rolls. Shake to coat. Place on lightly greased broiler pan. Discard excess flour mixture. Broil rolls 4 inches (10 cm) from heat for 3 to 4 minutes per side, turning to brown evenly. Place in ungreased 2 quart (2 L) casserole.

Combine water, consommé, onion, garlic and bay leaf in small bowl. Pour over rolls. Cover. Bake in 350°F (175°C) oven for 1 hour.

Stir second amount of water into second amount of flour in small cup until smooth. Stir into liquid in casserole. Bake for 15 minutes until sauce is thickened. Remove and discard bay leaf. Remove string or wooden picks before serving. Serves 8.

1 serving: 184 Calories; 6.4 g Total Fat; 417 mg Sodium; 22 g Protein; 9 g Carbohydrate; 1 g Dietary Fiber

Spaghetti Meat Sauce

This spicy, chunky sauce with little red and green flecks looks very appetizing.
Serve with hot spaghetti.

Lean ground beef	1 lb.	454 g
Medium onions, chopped	2	2
Celery ribs, chopped	2	2
Medium green pepper, chopped	1	1
Garlic clove, minced (or 1/4 tsp., 1 mL, powder)	1	1
Can of crushed tomatoes	14 oz.	398 mL
Can of diced tomatoes, with juice	28 oz.	796 mL
Water	1/3 cup	75 mL
Chopped fresh parsley (or 2 1/2 tsp., 12 mL, flakes)	3 tbsp.	50 mL
Dried whole oregano	1 tsp.	5 mL
Bay leaf	1	1
Chopped fresh sweet basil (or 3/4 tsp., 4 mL, dried)	1 tbsp.	15 mL
Salt	1/2 tsp.	2 mL
Granulated sugar	1/2 tsp.	2 mL
Dried crushed chilies	1 tsp.	5 mL
Freshly ground pepper, sprinkle		
Grated Parmesan cheese, for garnish		

Scramble-fry ground beef, onion, celery, green pepper and garlic in large saucepan until beef is no longer pink. Drain.

Add next 11 ingredients. Stir. Bring to a boil. Reduce heat. Simmer, uncovered, for 45 minutes until vegetables are soft and sauce is thickened. Remove and discard bay leaf.

Garnish individual servings with Parmesan cheese. Serves 6.

1 serving: 181 Calories; 7 g Total Fat; 601 mg Sodium; 16 g Protein; 15 g Carbohydrate; 3 g Dietary Fiber

Pictured on page 71.

Rolled Steak Florentine

An inexpensive company dish. Serve with wild and white rice and asparagus for a truly wonderful company dish.

Flank (or round) steak	2 1/4 lbs.	1 kg
Fresh (or frozen) spinach, cooked, squeezed dry and chopped	10 oz.	285 g
Fresh bread crumbs	3/4 cup	175 mL
Grated medium Cheddar cheese	1/2 cup	125 mL
Large egg, fork-beaten	1	1
Poultry seasoning	1/2 tsp.	2 mL
Salt	1/4 tsp.	1 mL
Pepper, to taste		
Can of tomato sauce	7 1/2 oz.	213 mL
Beef bouillon powder	1 tsp.	5 mL
Boiling water	1/2 cup	125 mL
Garlic clove, minced (or 1/4 tsp., 1 mL, powder)	1	1
Cold water	1/4 cup	60 mL
Cornstarch	1 tbsp.	15 mL

Cut steak into eight 3 x 4 inch (7.5 x 10 cm) pieces. Pound with mallet or rolling pin to 1/4 inch (6 mm) thickness.

Combine next 7 ingredients in large bowl. Mix well. Divide and spread evenly over surface of each steak. Roll up, jelly roll-style, starting with narrow edge. Tie with butcher's string or secure with metal skewers. Broil rolls 4 inches (10 cm) from heat, turning until nicely browned. Place in ungreased 3 quart (3 L) casserole.

Combine tomato sauce, bouillon powder, boiling water and garlic in small bowl. Pour over rolls. Cover. Bake in 350°F (175°C) oven for 1 1/2 hours, turning rolls after 1 hour, until tender. Remove rolls to warm platter. Pour liquid into small saucepan.

Stir cold water into cornstarch in small cup until smooth. Slowly stir into liquid. Heat and stir until thickened. Drizzle on sliced rolls. Serves 8.

1 serving: 312 Calories; 13.4 g Total Fat; 570 mg Sodium; 34 g Protein; 13 g Carbohydrate; 2 g Dietary Fiber

Pictured on front cover.

Goulash With Roasted Pepper

Substitute regular paprika for Hungarian for a slightly less pungent flavor.
Spoon over broad noodles or rice.

Inside round steak, cut across grain into thin strips	1 lb.	454 g
Olive (or cooking) oil	1 tsp.	5 mL
Medium onion, cut into slivers	1	1
Garlic clove, minced (or 1/4 tsp., 1 mL, powder)	1	1
Hungarian (or regular) paprika	1 1/2 tbsp.	25 mL
Large roma (plum) tomatoes, sliced	6	6
Can of condensed beef consommé	10 oz.	284 mL
Green, red or yellow Roasted Peppers, page 13, cut into strips	4	4
Salt	1/2 tsp.	2 mL
Freshly ground pepper, to taste		
Non-fat sour cream	2/3 cup	150 mL
All-purpose flour	2 tbsp.	30 mL

Sear beef strips in olive oil in large pot or Dutch oven on medium-high. Add onion, garlic and paprika. Heat, stirring often, for 8 to 10 minutes until onion is soft.

Add tomato and consommé. Cover. Reduce heat. Simmer for 1 hour until beef is tender.

Stir in pepper strips and salt. Sprinkle with pepper. Simmer, uncovered, for 15 minutes.

Stir sour cream into flour in small cup until smooth. Gradually stir into beef mixture. Heat and stir until boiling and thickened. Serves 4.

1 serving: 266 Calories; 6.5 g Total Fat; 808 mg Sodium; 30 g Protein; 24 g Carbohydrate; 4 g Dietary Fiber

Paré Pointer
Her favorite time where school is concerned is walking home.

Oriental Stuffed Meatloaf

A sweet treat inside and out. Best served the same day.

Lean ground beef	1 1/2 lbs.	680 g
Chopped green onion	1/2 cup	125 mL
Garlic clove, minced (or 1/4 tsp., 1 mL, powder)	1	1
Freshly grated gingerroot (or 1/2 tsp., 2 mL, ground ginger)	2 tsp.	10 mL
Large egg	1	1
Black bean (or soy) sauce	3 tbsp.	50 mL
Fresh white bread slices, processed into crumbs	3	3
Can of water chestnuts, drained and chopped	8 oz.	227 mL
Red Roasted Peppers, page 13, slivered	2	2
GLAZE		
Black bean (or soy) sauce	1/4 cup	60 mL
Pineapple juice (or water)	1/4 cup	60 mL
Cornstarch	1 tsp.	5 mL
Brown sugar, packed	1 tsp.	5 mL

Combine first 7 ingredients in large bowl. Mix well. Shape 1/2 of beef mixture into 12 x 5 inch (30 x 12.5 cm) rectangle on greased baking sheet.

Sprinkle with water chestnuts. Lay red pepper slivers not quite to edges of beef mixture. Shape remaining beef mixture into 12 x 5 inch (30 x 12.5 cm) rectangle on waxed paper. Invert onto pepper layer. Remove waxed paper. Pinch to seal edges. Shape into mound. Bake in 350°F (175°C) oven for 45 minutes until beef is no longer pink.

Glaze: Combine all 4 ingredients in small saucepan. Bring to a boil on medium. Reduce heat to medium-low. Simmer, uncovered, until slightly thickened. Remove meatloaf from oven. Brush glaze generously over meatloaf. Bake for 15 minutes until glaze is set. Cuts into 8 slices.

1 slice: 204 Calories; 8.7 g Total Fat; 395 mg Sodium; 18 g Protein; 13 g Carbohydrate; 1 g Dietary Fiber

Pineapple Meatloaf

A special meatloaf with a sweet tangy pineapple glaze.

Lean ground beef	2 lbs.	900 g
Fresh bread crumbs	2 cups	500 mL
Barbecue sauce	2/3 cup	150 mL
Large eggs	2	2
Salt	1 tsp.	5 mL
Pepper, sprinkle		
Can of pineapple slices, drained and juice reserved	19 oz.	540 mL
PINEAPPLE SAUCE		
Reserved pineapple juice		
Cornstarch	1 tbsp.	15 mL
Barbecue sauce	1/2 cup	125 mL
Whole green maraschino cherries, for garnish		

Combine ground beef, bread crumbs and barbecue sauce in large bowl. Stir well. Add eggs, salt and pepper. Mix well. Firmly pack beef mixture into greased 9 x 5 x 3 inch (22 x 12.5 x 7.5 cm) loaf pan. Bake in 350°F (175°C) oven for 1 hour. Drain.

Invert meatloaf onto ovenproof platter. Cut meatloaf into 10 slices, keeping slices upright. Insert pineapple slices between meatloaf slices.

Pineapple Sauce: Stir reserved pineapple juice into cornstarch in saucepan until smooth. Heat and stir until boiling, thickened and clear.

Add barbecue sauce. Stir to heat through. Baste meatloaf and pineapple slices with pineapple sauce.

Secure cherries on top of meatloaf slices using wooden picks. Bake for 15 minutes. Serve with remaining sauce. Serves 10.

1 serving: 238 Calories; 9.4 g Total Fat; 581 mg Sodium; 19 g Protein; 19 g Carbohydrate; 3 g Dietary Fiber

Paré Pointer

She was spooked about being a student after hearing about the school spirit.

Pesto Meatloaf Roll

Meatloaf with a mild pesto flavor. Serve with Fresh Tomato Salsa, page 15, for the perfect taste sensation.

Lean ground beef	1 1/2 lbs.	680 g
Fine dry bread crumbs	1 cup	250 mL
Large egg	1	1
Medium onion, finely chopped	1	1
Beef bouillon powder	2 tsp.	10 mL
Chopped sun-dried tomatoes, softened in boiling water for 10 minutes before chopping	1/2 cup	125 mL
Tomato paste	3 tbsp.	50 mL
Water	1/4 cup	60 mL
PESTO		
Fresh sweet basil, lightly packed	1 1/2 cups	375 mL
Pine nuts	6 tbsp.	100 mL
Garlic cloves, minced (or 3/4 tsp., 4 mL, powder)	3	3
Olive (or cooking) oil	6 tbsp.	100 mL
Grated Parmesan cheese	6 tbsp.	100 mL

Combine first 8 ingredients in large bowl. Mix well. Shape into 12 × 10 inch (30 × 25 cm) rectangle on greased foil.

Pesto: Measure all 5 ingredients into food processor. Process for 1 to 2 minutes until almost smooth. Spread pesto on beef mixture. Roll up, jelly roll-style, starting from long edge using foil as a guide and pulling foil back as you roll. Carefully place roll, seam side down, on ungreased baking sheet. Bake in 325°F (160°C) oven for 1 hour. Cuts into 8 slices.

1 slice: 372 Calories; 24.3 g Total Fat; 392 mg Sodium; 23 g Protein; 17 g Carbohydrate; 3 g Dietary Fiber

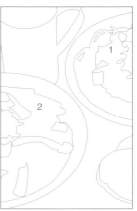

1. Spaghetti Meat Sauce, page 65
2. Penne With Wine Vegetable Sauce, page 61

Props Courtesy Of: Libicz's Kitchen Essentials

Entrées

Classic Meatloaf

For a zestier taste, use a vegetable cocktail juice such as V8,
instead of tomato juice.

Lean ground beef	1 1/2 lbs.	680 g
Quick-cooking rolled oats (not instant)	1 cup	250 mL
Finely chopped onion	1/4 cup	60 mL
Finely chopped celery	1/4 cup	60 mL
Finely chopped green pepper	1/4 cup	60 mL
Salt	1 1/2 tsp.	7 mL
Pepper	1/4 tsp.	1 mL
Ground sage	1/4 tsp.	1 mL
Large eggs, fork-beaten	2	2
Tomato juice	2/3 cup	150 mL

Combine all 10 ingredients in large bowl. Mix well. Firmly pack into ungreased 9 x 5 x 3 inch (22 x 12.5 x 7.5 cm) loaf pan. Bake in 350°F (175°C) oven for 1 1/4 hours. Let stand for 10 minutes before cutting. Cuts into 8 slices.

1 slice: 289 Calories; 15.5 g Total Fat; 652 mg Sodium; 21 g Protein; 16 g Carbohydrate; trace Dietary Fiber

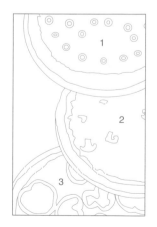

1. Greek Pizza, page 76
2. Easy Pizza, page 75
3. Traditional Pizza, page 74

Props Courtesy Of: Boston Pizza

Traditional Pizza

Every mouthful is filled with a burst of flavor.

Lean ground beef	1/2 lb.	225 g
Chopped onion	1 cup	250 mL
Sliced fresh mushrooms	2 cups	500 mL
Tomato paste	1/3 cup	75 mL
Italian-style flatbread (or pre-baked pizza crust), 12 inch, 30 cm, size	1	1
Dried sweet basil	1 tsp.	5 mL
Dried whole oregano	1/2 tsp.	2 mL
Grated part-skim mozzarella cheese	1 1/2 cups	375 mL
Grated Asiago cheese	1 cup	250 mL
Medium yellow pepper, cut into rings	1	1
Large tomato, seeded and diced	1	1

Scramble-fry ground beef and onion in non-stick frying pan until beef is no longer pink. Drain.

Add mushrooms. Cook until liquid from mushrooms is evaporated.

Spread thin layer of tomato paste on flatbread to edges. Sprinkle with basil and oregano. Layer beef mixture evenly over top. Sprinkle with both cheeses. Arrange yellow pepper rings over cheese. Sprinkle with tomato. Bake in 425°F (220°C) oven for 10 minutes until cheese is melted and crust is browned. Broil for 3 to 4 minutes until cheese is browned. Cuts into 8 wedges.

1 wedge: 319 Calories; 11.3 g Total Fat; 657 mg Sodium; 21 g Protein; 35 g Carbohydrate; 3 g Dietary Fiber

Pictured on page 72.

Pizza Loaf

Great to bake up for a luncheon or a teenage gathering.

Lean ground beef	1 1/2 lbs.	680 g
Can of spaghetti sauce	14 oz.	398 mL
Dried whole oregano	1 1/2 tsp.	7 mL
Chopped onion	1 cup	250 mL
Medium red pepper, chopped	1	1
Broccoli florets, cut into bite-sized pieces	2 cups	500 mL

(continued on next page)

French bread loaf, split	1	1
Grated part-skim mozzarella cheese	1 1/2 cups	375 mL
Grated medium Cheddar cheese	1 1/2 cups	375 mL

Scramble-fry ground beef in non-stick frying pan until no longer pink. Drain.

Combine beef, spaghetti sauce and oregano in medium bowl. Mix well. Set aside.

Stir-fry onion, red pepper and broccoli in same frying pan until tender-crisp.

Place loaf halves, cut sides up, on ungreased baking sheet. Spread beef mixture over each half. Sprinkle 1/2 of both cheeses over beef mixture. Top with broccoli mixture and remaining cheeses. Bake in 425°F (220°C) oven for 15 to 20 minutes until cheese is melted. Cuts into sixteen, 2 to 3 inch (5 to 7.5 cm) slices.

1 slice: 259 Calories; 11.3 g Total Fat; 437 mg Sodium; 17 g Protein; 23 g Carbohydrate; 1 g Dietary Fiber

Easy Pizza

Easy to prepare. Easy to assemble. Easy to devour.

Biscuit mix	2 cups	500 mL
Warm water	1/2 cup	125 mL
Olive (or cooking) oil	1 tbsp.	15 mL
Pizza (or spicy spaghetti) sauce	3/4 cup	175 mL
Lean ground beef, cooked and drained	1/2 lb.	225 g
Small onion, chopped	1	1
Dried whole oregano	1 tsp.	5 mL
Sliced fresh mushrooms	1 cup	250 mL
Grated part-skim mozzarella cheese	1 1/2 cups	375 mL
Chopped green pepper	1 cup	250 mL

Combine biscuit mix and warm water in medium bowl. Mix until dough forms a ball. Turn out onto lightly floured surface. Knead dough, adding enough biscuit mix, until a smooth ball forms that is no longer sticky.

Lightly grease 12 inch (30 cm) pizza pan and palms of your hands with olive oil. Press dough into pan forming rim around edge. Use more olive oil as needed.

Layer with remaining 7 ingredients in order given. Bake in 450°F (230°C) oven for 12 to 15 minutes until cheese is melted and crust is browned. Broil for 3 to 4 minutes until cheese is browned. Cuts into 8 wedges.

1 wedge: 323 Calories; 14.8 g Total Fat; 680 mg Sodium; 18 g Protein; 30 g Carbohydrate; 1 g Dietary Fiber

Pictured on page 72.

Greek Pizza

A great blend of beef, tomatoes, cheese and spices.

Lean ground beef	1/2 lb.	225 g
Garlic cloves, minced (or 1/2 tsp., 2 mL, powder)	2	2
Coarsely chopped onion	1 cup	250 mL
Frozen chopped spinach, thawed, squeezed dry and chopped further	10 oz.	300 g
Dried sweet basil	1 tsp.	5 mL
Lemon pepper	1/2 tsp.	2 mL
Chopped sun-dried tomatoes, softened in boiling water for 10 minutes before chopping	1/2 cup	125 mL
Unbaked pizza crust (12 inch, 30 cm, size) or pre-baked flatbread crust	1	1
Olive (or cooking) oil	1 tbsp.	15 mL
Crumbled feta cheese (about 3/4 cup, 175 mL)	4 oz.	113 g
Grated Parmesan cheese	1/4 cup	60 mL
Sliced ripe pitted olives	1/4 cup	60 mL

Scramble-fry ground beef, garlic and onion in non-stick frying pan until beef is no longer pink and onion is soft. Drain. Remove from heat.

Add spinach, basil, lemon pepper and tomato. Toss lightly.

Brush pizza crust with olive oil. Spread beef mixture over crust. Sprinkle with both cheeses and olives. Bake in 425°F (220°C) oven for 20 minutes if using unbaked pizza crust, or 10 minutes if using pre-baked crust, until cheese is melted and crust is browned. Cuts into 8 wedges.

1 wedge: 252 Calories; 9.8 g Total Fat; 785 mg Sodium; 14 g Protein; 28 g Carbohydrate; 3 g Dietary Fiber

Pictured on page 72.

Paré Pointer

The teacher was like a bird of prey. He watched his students like a hawk.

Greek Pita Pizzas

*A mild-tasting pizza that allows the feta and
spinach flavors to come through.*

Frozen chopped spinach	10 oz.	300 g
Lean ground beef	1 lb.	454 g
Garlic cloves, minced (or 1/2 tsp., 2 mL, powder)	2	2
Finely chopped onion	1/2 cup	125 mL
Salt	1/2 tsp.	2 mL
Freshly ground pepper	1/4 tsp.	1 mL
Dried whole oregano	1/2 tsp.	2 mL
Finely chopped fresh sweet basil (or 3/4 tsp., 4 mL, dried)	1 tbsp.	15 mL
Grated part-skim mozzarella cheese	1/2 cup	125 mL
Crumbled feta cheese (about 2.5 oz., 70 g)	1/2 cup	125 mL
Pitas (7 inch, 18 cm, size)	6	6
Medium tomatoes, seeded and diced	1 - 2	1 - 2
Crumbled feta cheese (about 2.5 oz., 70 g)	1/2 cup	125 mL
Sliced ripe pitted olives	1/2 cup	125 mL

Cook spinach according to package directions. Drain. Squeeze dry. Chop
into smaller pieces. Set aside.

Scramble-fry ground beef, garlic and onion in non-stick frying pan until
beef is no longer pink and onion is soft. Drain.

Add spinach and next 6 ingredients. Stir. Remove from heat.

Lay 3 pita breads on ungreased 11 × 17 inch (28 × 43 cm) baking sheet.
Flatten as best you can. Spread 1/2 cup (125 mL) beef mixture on each
pita. Sprinkle with 1/2 of tomato, second amount of feta cheese and olives.
Broil 4 to 6 inches (10 to 15 cm) from heat for 6 minutes until hot and
starting to brown on edges. Repeat with remaining pitas. Makes
6 individual pizzas.

*1 pizza: 505 Calories; 19.9 g Total Fat; 1208 mg Sodium; 32 g Protein; 50 g Carbohydrate;
3 g Dietary Fiber*

Entrées

Saucy Short Ribs

Just the right amount of sauce and distinctive vegetable taste.

Beef short ribs, bone-in, cut into serving-size pieces	3 lbs.	1.4 kg
Water	1/2 cup	125 mL
Large Spanish onion, sliced	1	1
Large green peppers, sliced	2	2
Fresh mushrooms, sliced	1 lb.	454 g
Chopped pimiento	1/4 cup	60 mL
Can of tomato paste	5 1/2 oz.	156 mL
All-purpose flour	2 tbsp.	30 mL
Cans of condensed beef broth (10 oz., 284 mL, each)	2	2
Dried whole oregano	1/2 tsp.	2 mL
Cayenne pepper	1/4 tsp.	1 mL
Worcestershire sauce	2 tbsp.	30 mL
Salt	1/4 tsp.	1 mL
Pepper	1/8 tsp.	0.5 mL

Place ribs in roasting pan. Add water. Cover. Bake in 350°F (175°C) oven for 2 hours. Drain.

Cover ribs with next 4 ingredients.

Combine remaining 8 ingredients in medium bowl. Mix well. Pour over ribs. Cover. Bake for 1 hour, stirring occasionally. Serves 6.

1 serving: 303 Calories; 12.8 g Total Fat; 693 mg Sodium; 31 g Protein; 17 g Carbohydrate; 3 g Dietary Fiber

Pictured on page 89.

 Freeze leftover canned broth or consommé in an airtight container for up to 6 months.

Sweet And Sour Short Ribs

Simply delicious with a nice, light sweet and sour flavor

Beef short ribs, bone in, cut in half crosswise	3 lbs.	1.4 kg
Boiling water	1 cup	250 mL
Finely chopped onion	1/4 cup	60 mL
Garlic clove, minced (or 1/4 tsp., 1 mL, powder)	1	1
Finely chopped celery	1/4 cup	60 mL
Finely chopped green pepper	1/2 cup	125 mL
Cooking oil	1 tsp.	5 mL
Pineapple juice	1 cup	250 mL
Water	1/2 cup	125 mL
Beef bouillon powder	2 tsp.	10 mL
Brown sugar, packed	1/4 cup	60 mL
White vinegar	1/2 cup	125 mL
Soy sauce	1 1/2 tbsp.	25 mL
Water	1/4 cup	60 mL
Cornstarch	1 tbsp.	15 mL

Place ribs in boiling water in large saucepan. Simmer for about 1 1/2 hours until beef is tender. Drain well. Transfer to ungreased shallow baking pan.

Sauté onion, garlic, celery and green pepper in cooking oil in frying pan until soft.

Add next 6 ingredients. Simmer for 5 minutes.

Stir third amount of water into cornstarch in small cup until smooth. Gradually pour into sauce. Heat and stir for 5 minutes until boiling and thickened. Pour sauce over ribs. Cover with foil. Bake in 350°F (175°C) oven for 20 minutes, turning ribs once. Remove foil. Turn ribs. Cook, uncovered, for 20 minutes. Serves 6.

1 serving: 296 Calories; 13 g Total Fat; 541 mg Sodium; 24 g Protein; 20 g Carbohydrate; 1 g Dietary Fiber

Pictured on page 89.

Entrées

79

Maple Short Ribs

A nice mild sweet flavor.

Beef short ribs, bone-in	3 lbs.	1.4 kg
Medium onion, sliced	1	1
Celery ribs, with leaves, coarsely chopped	2	2
Whole black peppercorns	10	10
Water, to cover		
Corn (or cane) syrup	1 1/2 cups	375 mL
Maple flavoring	1 tsp.	5 mL
Apple cider vinegar	1/4 cup	60 mL
Chili sauce	3 tbsp.	50 mL
Small onion, finely chopped	1	1
Worcestershire sauce	1 tsp.	5 mL
Dry mustard	3/4 tsp.	4 mL
Salt	1/2 tsp.	2 mL
Pepper	1/8 tsp.	0.5 mL

Place ribs, onion, celery and peppercorns in Dutch oven. Cover with water. Bring to a boil. Cover. Reduce heat. Simmer for 1 1/2 hours until ribs are tender. Remove ribs. Pat dry with paper towel. Discard liquid and vegetables. Arrange ribs in lightly greased shallow roasting pan.

Combine remaining 9 ingredients in medium bowl. Pour over ribs. Turn to coat. Bake, uncovered, in 325°F (160°C) oven for 30 minutes, basting occasionally. Serves 4.

1 serving: 513 Calories; 18.2 g Total Fat; 375 mg Sodium; 35 g Protein; 52 g Carbohydrate; 1 g Dietary Fiber

Pictured on page 89.

Dijon Meatballs

*Lots of creamy yellow sauce to serve over pasta
with a definite Dijon mustard flavor.*

MEATBALLS

Lean ground beef	1 lb.	454 g
Fresh bread crumbs	1/2 cup	125 mL
Finely chopped onion	1/4 cup	60 mL
Dijon mustard	1 tbsp.	15 mL
Salt	1/2 tsp.	2 mL
Pepper	1/4 tsp.	1 mL

SAUCE

All-purpose flour	3 tbsp.	50 mL
Cornstarch	1 tbsp.	15 mL
Beef bouillon powder	1 1/2 tsp.	7 mL
Water	1 cup	250 mL
Lemon juice	1 tsp.	5 mL
Milk	1 cup	250 mL
Finely chopped fresh chives	3 tbsp.	50 mL
Dijon mustard	2 tbsp.	30 mL
Freshly ground pepper	1/4 tsp.	1 mL

Meatballs: Combine all 6 ingredients in large bowl. Mix well. Shape into
1 1/2 inch (3.8 cm) balls. Arrange in single layer on ungreased baking
sheet. Bake in 400°F (205°C) oven for 20 minutes until browned.

Sauce: Combine flour, cornstarch, bouillon powder, water and lemon juice
in large saucepan until smooth. Stir in remaining 4 ingredients. Heat and
stir until boiling and thickened. Boil for 1 minute. Makes 2 1/4 cups
(550 mL) sauce. Add meatballs. Heat for 1 minute. Serves 4.

*1 serving: 264 Calories; 11.3 g Total Fat; 824 mg Sodium; 25 g Protein; 15 g Carbohydrate;
1 g Dietary Fiber*

Pictured on page 90.

Baked Meatballs In Wine

Subtle wine flavor with a pleasant blend of garlic and mushrooms.

MEATBALLS

Large eggs, fork-beaten	2	2
Fresh bread crumbs	3/4 cup	175 mL
Milk	1/3 cup	75 mL
Ground allspice	1/4 tsp.	1 mL
Salt	1 tsp.	5 mL
Pepper	1/8 tsp.	0.5 mL
Finely chopped onion	1/4 cup	60 mL
Lean ground beef	2 lbs.	900 g

WINE SAUCE

Small onion, finely chopped	1	1
Sliced fresh mushrooms	1 cup	250 mL
Garlic cloves, minced (or 1/2 tsp., 2 mL, powder)	2	2
Hard margarine (or butter)	2 tbsp.	30 mL
All-purpose flour	2 tbsp.	30 mL
Can of condensed beef consommé	10 oz.	284 mL
Dry red (or alcohol-free) wine	1/4 cup	60 mL

Chopped fresh parsley, for garnish

Meatballs: Combine all 8 ingredients in large bowl. Mix well. Shape into 1 1/2 inch (3.8 cm) balls. Arrange in single layer on large ungreased baking sheet. Bake in 500°F (260°C) oven for 10 to 12 minutes until browned. Place meatballs in ungreased 3 quart (3 L) casserole.

Wine Sauce: Sauté onion, mushrooms and garlic in margarine for 5 minutes until liquid is evaporated and onion is golden. Sprinkle with flour. Mix well. Slowly stir in consommé and wine. Heat and stir until boiling and thickened. Pour sauce over meatballs. Cover. Bake in 350°F (175°C) oven for 30 minutes.

Garnish with parsley. Serves 8.

1 serving: 261 Calories; 13.9 g Total Fat; 651 mg Sodium; 25 g Protein; 7 g Carbohydrate; 1 g Dietary Fiber

Pictured on page 90.

Honey Garlic Meatballs

You might also try this scrumptious sweet garlic sauce as a dip.

MEATBALLS

Lean ground beef	2 lbs.	900 g
Fresh white bread slices, processed into crumbs	4	4
Large eggs, fork-beaten	2	2
Salt	1 tsp.	5 mL
Cayenne pepper	1/4 tsp.	1 mL

SAUCE

Garlic cloves, minced	8	8
Hard margarine (or butter)	1 tbsp.	15 mL
Can of stewed tomatoes, with juice, puréed	14 oz.	398 mL
Liquid honey	3/4 cup	175 mL
Soy sauce	1/4 cup	60 mL
Cornstarch	2 tsp.	10 mL

Meatballs: Combine all 5 ingredients in large bowl. Mix well. Form into 1 1/2 inch (3.8 cm) balls. Arrange in single layer on ungreased baking sheet. Bake in 500°F (260°C) oven for 10 to 12 minutes until browned. Remove meatballs to ungreased 2 quart (2 L) casserole.

Sauce: Sauté garlic in margarine in medium saucepan until soft but not browned.

Add tomatoes and honey. Stir.

Stir soy sauce into cornstarch in small bowl until smooth. Stir into tomato mixture. Stir as you bring to a boil. Reduce heat. Simmer, uncovered, for 10 minutes, stirring frequently. Pour sauce over meatballs. Bake, uncovered, in 350°F (175°C) oven for 20 minutes until meatballs are glazed. Serves 8.

1 serving: 354 Calories; 12.6 g Total Fat; 1132 mg Sodium; 24 g Protein; 37 g Carbohydrate; 1 g Dietary Fiber

To freeze large quantities of meatballs ahead of time, arrange drained, cooked meatballs in a single layer on baking sheet. Freeze, uncovered, for about 1 hour until firm. Place in an airtight container. Freeze for up to 2 months.

Pepper Steak

The delicious sauce glazes the meat and vegetables. Most attractive.

Sirloin steak, 1/2 inch (12 mm) thick	1 lb.	454 g
Paprika	1 tbsp.	15 mL
Cooking oil	1 tbsp.	15 mL
Garlic cloves, minced (or 1/2 tsp., 2 mL, powder)	2	2
Can of condensed beef consommé	10 oz.	284 mL
Sliced green onion	1 cup	250 mL
Medium red pepper, cut into strips	1	1
Medium yellow pepper, cut into strips	1	1
Water	1/3 cup	75 mL
Soy sauce	1/4 cup	60 mL
Cornstarch	2 tbsp.	30 mL
Large tomatoes, cut into 8 wedges each	2	2

Pound steak to 1/4 inch (6 mm) thickness. Cut into 1/4 inch (6 mm) wide strips. Sprinkle with paprika. Let stand for 2 minutes.

Stir-fry beef strips in cooking oil in non-stick frying pan or wok until browned.

Add garlic. Sauté for 1 minute. Add consommé. Stir. Cover. Simmer for 30 minutes.

Stir in green onion and both peppers. Cover. Cook for 5 minutes.

Stir water and soy sauce into cornstarch in small cup until smooth. Gradually stir into beef mixture. Heat and stir for about 2 minutes until clear and thickened. Add tomato wedges. Stir gently to heat through. Serves 4.

1 serving: 247 Calories; 8.2 g Total Fat; 1489 mg Sodium; 29 g Protein; 15 g Carbohydrate; 2 g Dietary Fiber

Gourmet Stuffed Steak

Your guests will "ooh" and "aah" at the elegant presentation. Then they'll rave over how the vegetables, beef and gravy taste so delicious.

Flank steak	1 1/2 lbs.	680 g
MARINADE		
Red wine vinegar	1/2 cup	125 mL
Infused herb (or cooking) oil	2 tbsp.	30 mL
Garlic clove, minced (or 1/4 tsp., 1 mL, powder)	1	1

(continued on next page)

Entrées

STUFFING

Fresh (or frozen, thawed) spinach, cooked, squeezed dry and chopped	5 oz.	140 g
Medium carrots, blanched and cut in half lengthwise	2	2
Small onions, blanched and sliced	2	2
Hard-boiled eggs, quartered	2	2
Medium red pepper, sliced	1	1
Chopped fresh parsley (or 1 1/2 tsp., 7 mL, flakes)	2 tbsp.	30 mL
Salt	1/4 tsp.	1 mL
Pepper	1/8 tsp.	0.5 mL

GRAVY

Beef bouillon powder	2 tbsp.	30 mL
Boiling water	4 cups	1 L
Cold water	1 cup	250 mL
All-purpose flour	1/4 cup	60 mL
Salt	1/4 tsp.	1 mL
Freshly ground pepper	1/8 tsp.	0.5 mL

Butterfly steak by cutting horizontally lengthwise, not quite through center to within 1/2 inch (12 mm) from edge. Open flat. Pound with mallet or rolling pin to 1/4 inch (6 mm) thickness.

Marinade: Combine all 3 ingredients in small bowl. Place steak in shallow dish or resealable freezer bag. Pour marinade over steak. Turn to coat. Cover or seal. Marinate in refrigerator for 6 hours or overnight, turning once. Remove steak. Discard marinade.

Stuffing: Layer all 8 ingredients, in order given, evenly over steak, leaving about 3 inch (7.5 cm) uncovered flap from 1 edge. Roll, jelly roll-style, ending with exposed steak, folding it over edges. Tie with butcher's string or secure with metal skewers. Broil 4 inches (10 cm) from heat for 4 minutes per side, turning until evenly browned. Place in medium roasting pan. Do not place on rack.

Gravy: Combine bouillon powder and boiling water in large bowl. Stir. Pour over roll. Cover. Bake in 350°F (175°C) oven for 1 1/2 hours, turning once so that top does not dry out. Remove roll. Let stand for 10 minutes before slicing. Measure 3 cups (750 mL) liquid left in roasting pan. Discard remaining liquid. Spoon off any fat from measured amount. Return liquid to roasting pan.

Stir cold water into flour in small cup until smooth. Gradually stir into liquid. Heat and stir until boiling and thickened. Add second amounts of salt and pepper. Serve with sliced roll. Serves 6.

1 serving: 280 Calories; 11.9 g Total Fat; 1210 mg Sodium; 30 g Protein; 13 g Carbohydrate; 2 g Dietary Fiber

Beef In Pastry

Fussy but fast. Mild-tasting tender beef in a golden packet. Simply wonderful!

Fresh mushrooms, finely chopped	1/2 lb.	225 g
Olive (or cooking) oil	2 tsp.	10 mL
Dry red (or alcohol-free) wine	3 tbsp.	50 mL
Finely chopped green onion	1/4 cup	60 mL
Dried thyme	1/4 tsp.	1 mL
Salt	1/4 tsp.	1 mL
Pepper	1/8 tsp.	0.5 mL
Beef tenderloin steaks (4 oz., 113 g, each), 1 inch (2.5 cm) thick	4	4
Salt, sprinkle		
Pepper, sprinkle		
Frozen phyllo pastry sheets, thawed according to package directions	6	6

Sauté mushrooms in olive oil in frying pan until tender. Add wine. Stir. Cook for 2 minutes until liquid is evaporated.

Add green onion, thyme and first amounts of salt and pepper. Stir. Remove mixture from frying pan. Cool thoroughly.

Sear steaks, in same frying pan, on medium-high, for 1 1/2 minutes per side. Steaks will only be partially cooked. Do not overcook. Sprinkle with second amounts of salt and pepper.

Spray each phyllo sheet thoroughly with cooking spray. Stack into 1 pile on flat surface. Cut lengthwise in half and then crosswise in half to make 4 equal portions. Divide mushroom mixture among 4 portions. Spread slightly in center to diameter of each steak. Place steaks on mushroom mixture. Bring all 4 corners of phyllo together. Pinch and twist tightly to close. Lightly spray each "packet" with cooking spray. Place on lightly greased baking sheet. Bake in 425°F (220°C) oven for 9 to 10 minutes until golden. Let stand for 5 minutes. Serve immediately. Serves 4.

1 serving: 318 Calories; 17.1 g Total Fat; 362 mg Sodium; 25 g Protein; 13 g Carbohydrate; 1 g Dietary Fiber

Royal Rib-Eye

This very tender roast is enhanced by the rosemary and wine.

Boneless rib-eye roast	4 lbs.	1.8 kg
Salt	1 tsp.	5 mL
Freshly ground pepper	1/4 tsp.	1 mL
Dried rosemary, crushed	1/2 tsp.	2 mL
Bacon slices, cut in half	6	6
Medium-dry red (or alcohol-free) wine	1/2 cup	125 mL
Large fresh mushrooms (or 8 slices portobello mushrooms)	1 lb.	454 g
Hard margarine (or butter)	1/4 cup	60 mL

Sprinkle roast with salt, pepper and rosemary. Lay bacon slices over roast. Place on rack in shallow roasting pan. Roast, uncovered, in 450°F (230°C) oven for 30 minutes. Remove from oven. Remove and discard string and bacon. Reduce temperature to 300°F (150°C).

Pour wine over roast. Roast, uncovered, for 50 to 60 minutes until meat thermometer registers 140°F (60°C) for rare. Remove from oven. Strain, reserving liquid. Spoon off fat. Tent roast with foil. Let stand for 15 minutes before carving.

Sauté mushrooms in margarine in frying pan for about 5 minutes until soft and browned. Slice roast into 1/2 to 3/4 inch (12 to 20 mm) pieces. Arrange on warmed platter. Surround with mushrooms. Pour reserved liquid over roast. Serves 12.

1 serving: 422 Calories; 30.3 g Total Fat; 378 mg Sodium; 32 g Protein; 2 g Carbohydrate; 1 g Dietary Fiber

 To determine the doneness for dry heat and moist heat methods of cooking roasts, use a meat thermometer. Insert thermometer into center of roast, avoiding any bone or fat.

Savory Rib Roast

In each bite you can taste the flavorful spices.

Standing rib roast	6 lbs.	2.7 kg
Ground thyme	1 tbsp.	15 mL
Dried rosemary, crushed	1 tsp.	5 mL
Ground sage	1 tsp.	5 mL
Salt	1 tsp.	5 mL
Freshly ground pepper	1 tsp.	5 mL

Place roast, fat side up, on rack in large roasting pan.

Combine remaining 5 ingredients in small bowl. Rub all over roast. Roast, uncovered, in 325°F (160°C) oven for 35 minutes per lb. (75 minutes per kg) for rare, 45 minutes per lb. (100 minutes per kg) for medium, 55 minutes per lb. (120 minutes per kg) for well-done. Let stand for 10 minutes before carving. Serves 12.

1 serving: 237 Calories; 11.6 g Total Fat; 303 mg Sodium; 31 g Protein; 1 g Carbohydrate; trace Dietary Fiber

Pictured on page 107.

1. Maple Short Ribs, page 80
2. Saucy Short Ribs, page 78
3. Sweet And Sour Short Ribs, page 79

Ruby-Glazed Roast Beef

A beautifully done roast with the addition of a mild sweet glaze.

Inside round (or eye of round) roast	3 lbs.	1.4 kg
Red currant jelly	1 cup	250 mL
Ground ginger	1/2 tsp.	2 mL
Chopped sun-dried tomatoes, softened in boiling water for 10 minutes before chopping	1/4 cup	60 mL
Italian no-salt seasoning (such as Mrs. Dash)	1 tsp.	5 mL
Water	1/4 cup	60 mL
Cornstarch	1 tbsp.	15 mL

Place roast, fat side up, on rack in small roasting pan. Roast, uncovered, in 500°F (260°C) oven for 30 minutes. Reduce temperature to 275°F (140°C).

Heat next 4 ingredients in small saucepan. Pour over roast. Roast, uncovered, for 25 minutes per lb. (55 minutes per kg), basting several times with sauce, until meat thermometer registers 160°F (75°C) for medium. Remove roast from oven. Tent with foil.

Stir water into cornstarch in small cup until smooth. Gradually stir into liquid in pan. Heat and stir until boiling and thickened. Serve with roast. Serves 8.

1 serving: 346 Calories; 8 g Total Fat; 111 mg Sodium; 34 g Protein; 34 g Carbohydrate; 2 g Dietary Fiber

Pictured on page 107.

1. Dijon Meatballs, page 81
2. Baked Meatballs In Wine, page 82

Eye Of The Orient

Teriyaki flavor throughout this easy-to-slice roast. Add water to prevent scorching.

MARINADE

Prepared orange juice	1/2 cup	125 mL
Sherry	1/2 cup	125 mL
Soy sauce	1/4 cup	60 mL
Freshly grated gingerroot (or 1/2 tsp., 2 mL, ground ginger)	2 tsp.	10 mL
Finely chopped onion	1/4 cup	60 mL
Brown sugar, packed	2 tbsp.	30 mL
Beef bouillon powder	1 tbsp.	15 mL
Garlic clove, minced (or 1/4 tsp., 1 mL, powder)	1	1
Eye of round roast	2 lbs.	900 g
Water	1 cup	250 mL

Marinade: Combine all 8 ingredients in medium bowl. Place roast in deep bowl or resealable freezer bag. Pour marinade over roast. Turn to coat. Cover or seal. Marinate in refrigerator for 8 to 10 hours or overnight, turning several times. Remove roast, reserving marinade. Place roast on rack in medium roasting pan. Roast, uncovered, in 500°F (260°C) oven for 30 minutes.

Add water to pan. Reduce heat to 275°F (140°C). Roast, uncovered, for about 1 1/4 hours until meat thermometer registers 160°F (75°C) for medium. Strain reserved marinade into saucepan. Bring to a boil. Boil for 2 minutes. Use as is or thicken with 2 tsp. (10 mL) cornstarch mixed with 1/4 cup (60 mL) water. Serves 8.

1 serving: 184 Calories; 5.5 g Total Fat; 792 mg Sodium; 23 g Protein; 7 g Carbohydrate; trace Dietary Fiber

Herbed Beef Tenderloin

Use any leftover tenderloin the next day in sandwiches.

Tenderloin roast	3 lbs.	1.4 kg
Olive (or cooking) oil	2 tsp.	10 mL

(continued on next page)

Dried thyme	1 1/2 tsp.	7 mL
Dried tarragon	1 tsp.	5 mL
Garlic powder	1/2 tsp.	2 mL
Onion powder	1 tsp.	5 mL
Freshly ground pepper	1 tsp.	5 mL
Salt	1/4 tsp.	1 mL
Parsley flakes	2 tsp.	10 mL

If necessary, tuck thin end of roast underneath to make shape as uniform as possible. Tie tenderloin lengthwise and then crosswise with butcher's string to hold. Rub olive oil over entire surface of roast to coat lightly.

Combine remaining 7 ingredients in small cup. Spread on piece of waxed paper. Shake paper to spread evenly. Press roast down onto seasoning mixture to coat evenly. Place roast on rack in broiler pan. Roast, uncovered, in 425°F (220°C) oven for 45 minutes until meat thermometer registers 140°F (60°C) for rare or 160°F (75°C) for medium. Remove from oven. Tent roast with foil. Let stand for 15 minutes before carving. Serves 8.

1 serving: 218 Calories; 11.2 g Total Fat; 145 mg Sodium; 27 g Protein; 1 g Carbohydrate; trace Dietary Fiber

Cranberry Roast

Combination of tart and sweet topped with a noticeable ginger presence.

Eye of round (or inside round or sirloin tip) roast	4 lbs.	1.8 kg
Jellied cranberry sauce	14 oz.	398 mL
Green onions, finely chopped	2	2
Soy sauce	1/4 cup	60 mL
Freshly grated gingerroot (or 1 1/2 tsp., 7 mL, ground ginger)	2 tbsp.	30 mL

Place roast, fat side up, in bottom of medium roasting pan. Do not place on rack. Roast, uncovered, in 500°F (260°C) oven for 30 minutes.

Combine cranberry sauce, onion, soy sauce and ginger in large saucepan. Heat and stir on medium until smooth. Pour over roast, allowing it to drizzle down all sides. Roast, uncovered, in 275°F (140°C) oven for 25 minutes per lb. (55 minutes per kg), basting each hour, until meat thermometer registers 160°F (75°C) for medium. Serves 12.

1 serving: 261 Calories; 7.6 g Total Fat; 422 mg Sodium; 31 g Protein; 16 g Carbohydrate; trace Dietary Fiber

Pictured on page 108.

Garlic Roast And Veggies

Stir vegetables occasionally to keep moist. A beautiful medley of color.
The Italian-seasoned vegetables are the perfect complement to this garlic roast.

Sirloin roast	2 1/2 lbs.	1.1 kg
Garlic cloves, slivered	2	2
Dried sweet basil	1 tsp.	5 mL
Dried whole oregano	1 tsp.	5 mL
Freshly ground pepper, sprinkle		
Large garlic bulb	1	1
Medium baking potatoes, quartered	3	3
Medium carrots, sliced diagonally 1/2 inch (12 mm) thick	2	2
Medium onions, quartered	3	3
Low-fat Italian dressing	3 tbsp.	50 mL
Medium red pepper, quartered	1	1
Medium yellow pepper, quartered	1	1
Medium zucchini, with peel, sliced diagonally 3/4 inch (2 cm) thick	2	2
Low-fat Italian dressing	3 tbsp.	50 mL

Make small slits at regular intervals over surface of roast with sharp knife. Insert garlic slivers into slits.

Combine basil, oregano and pepper in small cup. Spread on piece of waxed paper. Shake paper to spread evenly. Press roast, top end down, onto seasoning mixture. Place roast, seasoned end up, on rack in medium roasting pan.

Cut stem end of garlic bulb to slice through each clove. Wrap bulb securely in foil. Place in pan.

Combine next 4 ingredients in large bowl. Arrange around roast. Roast, uncovered, in 325°F (160°C) oven for 30 to 40 minutes per lb. (85 to 110 minutes per kg) until meat thermometer registers 160°F (75°C) for medium. Remove roast to platter. Tent with foil. Let stand until vegetables are done.

Combine both peppers, zucchini and second amount of Italian dressing. Add to vegetables in roasting pan. Increase temperature to 425°F (220°C). Roast, uncovered, for 20 minutes until zucchini is tender-crisp. Remove foil-wrapped garlic. Squeeze garlic through cut end over vegetables. Gently toss to combine. Serves 8.

1 serving: 269 Calories; 6 g Total Fat; 241 mg Sodium; 32 g Protein; 22 g Carbohydrate; 4 g Dietary Fiber

Tangy Beef Roast

Appropriately named, this roast has a sharp lemon and mustard edge.

MARINADE

Lemon juice	1/2 cup	125 mL
Cooking oil	2 tbsp.	30 mL
Dry mustard	1 tbsp.	15 mL
Chopped fresh sweet basil (or 3/4 tsp., 4 mL, dried)	1 tbsp.	15 mL
Salt	1/2 tsp.	2 mL
Pepper	1/4 tsp.	1 mL
Garlic cloves, minced (or 1/2 tsp., 2 mL, powder)	2	2
Sirloin tip (or round or rump) roast	4 1/2 lbs.	2 kg

HORSERADISH SPREAD

Prepared horseradish	1/2 cup	125 mL
Dry mustard	1 tsp.	5 mL

Marinade: Combine first 7 ingredients in small bowl. Place roast in deep bowl or large resealable freezer bag. Pour marinade over roast. Turn to coat. Cover or seal. Marinate in refrigerator overnight, turning several times. Remove roast. Discard marinade. Place roast on rack in broiler pan. Roast, uncovered, in 500°F (260°C) oven for 30 minutes. Reduce temperature to 275°F (140°C). Roast, uncovered, for 25 minutes per lb. (55 minutes per kg) until meat thermometer registers 150°F (65°C) for medium-rare.

Horseradish Spread: Combine horseradish and mustard in small bowl. Mix well. Serve with roast. Serves 12.

1 serving: 219 Calories; 9.9 g Total Fat; 97 mg Sodium; 30 g Protein; 1 g Carbohydrate; trace Dietary Fiber

Pictured on page 108.

 To save time during the week, prepare and cook roasts on the weekend when you have more time. Cook to medium doneness, internal temperature of 160°F (75°C). Then slice, wrap airtight and chill, ready for serving for weekday suppers or for sandwiches.

Beef Tabbouleh

Very colorful and flavorful salad.

Bulgur	1 cup	250 mL
Boiling water	2 cups	500 mL
Roma (plum) tomatoes, seeded and diced	2	2
Very thinly sliced red onion	1/2 cup	125 mL
Finely chopped fresh mint leaves	1/4 cup	60 mL
Finely chopped fresh parsley (or 2 1/2 tsp., 12 mL, flakes)	3 tbsp.	50 mL
Green onions, finely chopped	2	2
Finely chopped cooked lean beef	1 cup	250 mL
Olive (or cooking) oil	1 tbsp.	15 mL
Lemon juice	3 tbsp.	50 mL
Ground cumin	1/4 tsp.	1 mL
Ground coriander	1/4 tsp.	1 mL
Hot pepper sauce	1/8 tsp.	0.5 mL
Salt	1 tsp.	5 mL
Lemon pepper	1/4 tsp.	1 mL

Place bulgur in small bowl. Pour boiling water over top. Let stand for 30 minutes. Drain off any excess water.

Combine remaining 13 ingredients in large bowl. Add bulgur. Toss. Chill for 30 minutes to blend flavors. Serves 6.

1 serving: 169 Calories; 4.2 g Total Fat; 481 mg Sodium; 11 g Protein; 24 g Carbohydrate; 6 g Dietary Fiber

Apple And Beef Salad

Dressing has a nice dill flavor and the crunchy apples are a delightful addition.

Cooked lean beef, cut into 1/2 inch (12 mm) cubes	3 cups	750 mL
Cubed cooked potato	3 cups	750 mL
Finely chopped celery	1/2 cup	125 mL
Medium green pepper, finely chopped	1	1
Grated Colby cheese	1 cup	250 mL
Medium apples, diced into 1/2 inch (12 mm) pieces	2	2
Lemon juice	1 tsp.	5 mL

(continued on next page)

DILL DRESSING

Light salad dressing (or mayonnaise)	1/2 cup	125 mL
Milk	1/4 cup	60 mL
Dill weed	1 tsp.	5 mL
Salt	1/2 tsp.	2 mL
Pepper, sprinkle		
Paprika, for garnish		

Combine first 5 ingredients in large bowl.

Combine apple and lemon juice in small bowl. Toss. Add to beef mixture.

Dill Dressing: Combine first 5 ingredients in small bowl. Add to beef mixture. Toss gently.

Sprinkle with paprika. Serves 6.

1 serving: 374 Calories; 17.1 g Total Fat; 551 mg Sodium; 28 g Protein; 27 g Carbohydrate; 2 g Dietary Fiber

---

Peachy Beef Salad

Uses leftover cooked beef. Quick to prepare.

Can of sliced peaches, drained and juice reserved	14 oz.	398 mL
Head of romaine lettuce, torn into bite-sized pieces	1	1
Strips of cooked lean beef	1 1/2 cups	375 mL
Medium-ripe avocado, sliced	1	1

DRESSING

Low-fat Italian dressing	1/4 cup	60 mL
Sweet and sour barbecue sauce	2 tbsp.	30 mL
Reserved peach juice	1/4 cup	60 mL
Freshly ground pepper, sprinkle		

Cherry tomatoes, halved (for garnish)
Sliced almonds, toasted (see Tip, page 27), for garnish

Toss peaches, lettuce, beef strips and avocado in large bowl.

Dressing: Combine first 4 ingredients in small bowl. Pour over lettuce mixture. Toss lightly.

Garnish with tomatoes and almonds. Serves 6.

1 serving: 167 Calories; 7.6 g Total Fat; 221 mg Sodium; 13 g Protein; 13 g Carbohydrate; 3 g Dietary Fiber

Mango Tango Salad

This salad is sweet, slightly tangy, and is for mango lovers.
Beef is flavored by the red wine.

Inside round (or sirloin tip) steak	1 lb.	454 g
Dry red wine	1/2 cup	125 mL
Penne (or fusilli or rigatoni) pasta, uncooked	2 cups	500 mL
Hot mango chutney	1 cup	250 mL
Cooking oil	2 tsp.	10 mL
Sesame (or cooking) oil	1 tsp.	5 mL
Lemon juice	1/4 cup	60 mL
Frozen peas	1 1/2 cups	375 mL
Large carrot, cut julienne	1	1
Diced ripe mango	1/2 cup	125 mL
Sesame seeds, toasted (see Tip, page 27)	2 tbsp.	30 mL

Place steak in shallow dish or resealable freezer bag. Pour wine over steak. Turn to coat. Cover or seal. Marinate in refrigerator for at least 2 hours, turning several times. Remove steak. Discard wine. Place steak on rack in broiler pan. Broil for 5 to 6 minutes per side until desired doneness. Thinly slice steak across grain.

Cook pasta according to package directions. Drain. Rinse under cold water. Drain well.

Combine next 7 ingredients in large bowl. Add steak and pasta. Toss. Chill for 3 to 4 hours to blend flavors.

Add sesame seeds just before serving. Toss. Serves 4.

1 serving: 504 Calories; 10.9 g Total Fat; 118 mg Sodium; 33 g Protein; 68 g Carbohydrate; 6 g Dietary Fiber

 If being browned first, medium tender and less tender cuts of beef should not be salted as salt will draw out needed moisture.

Summertime Salad

A pretty luncheon salad. The dressing can be made the day before.

Julienned strips of cooked lean beef	3 cups	750 mL
Sliced green beans, steamed	1 cup	250 mL
Sliced English cucumber, with peel	1/2 cup	125 mL
Diced celery	1 1/2 cups	375 mL
Diced green pepper	1/2 cup	125 mL
Baby potatoes, boiled and diced	1 lb.	454 g
Finely chopped green onion	1/4 cup	60 mL
Chopped fresh parsley (or 2 1/2 tsp., 12 mL, flakes)	3 tbsp.	50 mL
BALSAMIC DRESSING		
Olive (or cooking) oil	1/3 cup	75 mL
Balsamic vinegar	2 tbsp.	30 mL
Salt	3/4 tsp.	4 mL
Garlic clove, minced (or 1/4 tsp., 1 mL, powder)	1	1
Dijon mustard	1 1/2 tsp.	7 mL
Dried tarragon	1/4 tsp.	1 mL
Mixed salad greens	6 cups	1.5 L
Chopped fresh parsley, for garnish		
Tomatoes, cut into wedges, for garnish		
Hard-boiled eggs, sliced, for garnish		

Combine first 8 ingredients in large bowl. Toss.

Balsamic Dressing: Combine first 6 ingredients in small bowl. Pour over vegetable mixture. Toss. Chill for at least 1 hour to blend flavors.

Serve on a bed of salad greens. Garnish with parsley, tomato and egg. Serves 6.

1 serving: 291 Calories; 16.4 g Total Fat; 407 mg Sodium; 23 g Protein; 14 g Carbohydrate; 2 g Dietary Fiber

Steak 'N' Veggie Pasta Salad

An unusual salad containing steak that has been marinated ahead of time.

MARINADE

Olive (or cooking) oil	1 tbsp.	15 mL
Red wine vinegar	1 tbsp.	15 mL
Condensed beef broth	1 tbsp.	15 mL
Garlic cloves, minced (or 1/2 tsp., 2 mL, powder)	2	2
Freshly ground pepper, sprinkle		
Inside round (or sirloin tip) steak	1 1/2 lbs.	680 g
Rotini pasta, uncooked	2 cups	500 mL
Small cauliflower florets	1/2 cup	125 mL
Small broccoli florets	1/2 cup	125 mL
Carrots, cut julienne	2	2
Boiling water		
Green onions, thinly sliced	2	2
Small green pepper, cut julienne	1	1
Small red pepper, cut julienne	1	1
Low-fat Italian (or Caesar) dressing	1 cup	250 mL
Salt	1/2 tsp.	2 mL
Freshly ground pepper, sprinkle		
Grated Parmesan cheese, for garnish		

Marinade: Combine first 5 ingredients in small bowl.

Place steak in shallow dish or resealable freezer bag. Pour marinade over steak. Turn to coat. Cover or seal. Marinate in refrigerator for 8 hours or overnight, turning several times. Remove steak. Discard marinade. Place steak on rack in broiler pan. Broil for 4 to 5 minutes per side until desired doneness. Cool completely. Thinly slice steak across grain.

Cook pasta according to package directions. Drain. Rinse in cold water. Drain well.

Add cauliflower, broccoli and carrot to boiling water in medium saucepan. Boil for 3 minutes. Drain. Immediately cool in ice water. Drain. Pat dry.

Combine steak, pasta, blanched vegetables, onion and both peppers in large bowl. Drizzle with dressing. Add salt and pepper. Toss. Marinate in refrigerator for at least 1 hour to blend flavors.

Sprinkle with Parmesan cheese. Serves 6.

1 serving: 306 Calories; 8.3 g Total Fat; 899 mg Sodium; 27 g Protein; 30 g Carbohydrate; 2 g Dietary Fiber

Kiwi, Beef And Pasta Salad

Serve this unique tropical, light, summery salad warm or cold.

MARINADE

Ripe kiwifruit, peeled and mashed	3	3
Lime juice	1/3 cup	75 mL
Water	1/3 cup	75 mL
Granulated sugar	1 tbsp.	15 mL
Garlic cloves, minced (or 1/2 tsp., 2 mL, powder)	2	2
Small onion, finely chopped	1	1
Gingerroot, 1 inch (2.5 cm) piece, finely chopped	1	1
Dried tarragon	1 tsp.	5 mL
Salt	1/2 tsp.	2 mL
Lemon pepper	1 tsp.	5 mL
Inside round (or sirloin tip) steak, 3/4 inch (2 cm) thick	1 lb.	454 g
Fusilli pasta (or large pasta shells), uncooked	3 cups	750 mL
Cherry tomatoes, halved	12	12

Kiwifruit, peeled and sliced, for garnish
Star fruit, sliced, for garnish

Marinade: Combine first 10 ingredients in small bowl. Stir well.

Place steak in shallow dish or resealable freezer bag. Pour marinade over steak. Turn to coat. Cover or seal. Marinate in refrigerator for 30 to 45 minutes, turning once. Remove steak, reserving marinade. Thinly slice steak across grain. Sear steak in non-stick frying pan. Place marinade in small saucepan. Bring to a boil. Boil for 5 minutes.

Cook pasta according to package directions. Drain. Rinse in cold water. Drain well.

Combine pasta, marinade and tomatoes in large bowl. Toss. Arrange steak over pasta mixture.

Garnish with kiwifruit and star fruit. Serves 4.

1 serving: 346 Calories; 5.2 g Total Fat; 399 mg Sodium; 29 g Protein; 46 g Carbohydrate; 4 g Dietary Fiber

Minty Beef Salad

Fresh looking and fresh tasting. Summer all year round.

LIME DRESSING

Freshly grated lime peel (about 2 medium)	2 tbsp.	30 mL
Freshly squeezed lime juice (about 2 medium)	1/2 cup	125 mL
Freshly grated gingerroot (or 2 1/2 tsp., 12 mL, ground ginger)	3 tbsp.	50 mL
Chopped fresh cilantro (or fresh parsley)	2 tbsp.	30 mL
Fresh mint leaves, packed	1 cup	250 mL
Brown sugar, packed	1 tsp.	5 mL
Soy sauce	1 tbsp.	15 mL
Water	1/2 cup	125 mL
Olive (or cooking) oil	1/4 cup	60 mL
Sesame (or cooking) oil	1/2 tsp.	2 mL
Sirloin steak	3/4 lb.	340 g
Heads of butter lettuce, torn	2	2
Fresh bean sprouts	1 cup	250 mL
Cubed ripe cantaloupe	2 cups	500 mL
Coarsely chopped salted peanuts	1/2 cup	125 mL

Mint leaves, for garnish

Lime Dressing: Place all 10 ingredients in blender. Process until almost smooth.

Place steak in shallow dish or resealable freezer bag. Pour 1/2 of dressing over steak. Turn to coat. Cover or seal. Marinate in refrigerator for 30 minutes, turning once. Remove steak. Discard marinade. Place steak on rack in broiler pan. Broil for 5 minutes per side until desired doneness. Cool. Thinly slice steak across grain.

Combine lettuce, bean sprouts, cantaloupe and peanuts in large bowl. Pour remaining dressing over top. Toss to coat. Arrange steak over top.

Garnish with mint leaves. Serves 4.

1 serving: 375 Calories; 22.9 g Total Fat; 439 mg Sodium; 26 g Protein; 21 g Carbohydrate; 2 g Dietary Fiber

Pictured on front cover.

Artichoke Toss

Colorful and unique combination of beef, peppers and artichokes.
Serve warm or cold.

Low-fat French dressing	1/2 cup	125 mL
Cooking oil	2 tbsp.	30 mL
Garlic cloves, minced (or 1/2 tsp., 2 mL, powder)	2	2
Ground cumin	1 tsp.	5 mL
Sirloin (or strip loin or inside round) steak	1 lb.	454 g
Sliced fresh mushrooms	1/2 cup	125 mL
Small red pepper, cut into slivers	1	1
Small yellow pepper, cut into slivers	1	1
Can of artichoke hearts, drained and quartered	14 oz.	398 mL
Green leaf lettuce leaves	4 - 8	4 - 8

Combine first 4 ingredients in small bowl. Stir well. Reserve 1/4 cup (60 mL).

Place steak in shallow dish or resealable freezer bag. Pour remaining dressing mixture over steak. Turn to coat. Cover or seal. Marinate in refrigerator for 1 1/2 hours. Remove steak. Discard marinade. Place steak on rack in broiler pan. Broil for 5 to 6 minutes per side until desired doneness. Thinly slice steak across grain.

Combine mushrooms, both peppers and reserved dressing mixture in small bowl. Place on broiler pan. Broil for 2 minutes.

Place artichokes in medium bowl. Add mushroom mixture. Toss.

Arrange lettuce leaves on individual plates or line shallow bowl. Top with steak and artichoke mixture. Serves 4.

1 serving: 242 Calories; 9.7 g Total Fat; 456 mg Sodium; 26 g Protein; 14 g Carbohydrate; 1 g Dietary Fiber

---

Paré Pointer
His music instructor asked him to sing higher so he climbed a ladder.

Beef Benedict

Beautiful to look at and delicious to eat.

Béarnaise Sauce, page 13	1/4 cup	60 mL
Rib-eye (or sirloin) steak	4 oz.	113 g
English muffin, toasted	1/2	1/2
Large egg, poached	1	1
Paprika, sprinkle		

Prepare Béarnaise Sauce. Keep warm.

Broil, grill or pan-fry steak to desired doneness. Cut into thin strips. Pile onto English muffin. Top with egg and Béarnaise Sauce. Sprinkle with paprika. Serves 1.

1 serving: 381 Calories; 11.4 g Total Fat; 514 mg Sodium; 37 g Protein; 30 g Carbohydrate; 1 g Dietary Fiber

Speedy Fajitas

Fast, flavorful and fun. The perfect lunch.

Lime juice	1 tbsp.	15 mL
Chili powder	1 tbsp.	15 mL
Dried whole oregano	1 tsp.	5 mL
Garlic powder	1/2 tsp.	2 mL
Freshly ground pepper, sprinkle		
Beef stir-fry strips	1 lb.	454 g
Sliced fresh mushrooms	2 cups	500 mL
Medium red (or green) pepper, cut into strips	1	1
Green onions, cut into 1 inch (2.5 cm) pieces	4	4
Cooking oil	2 tsp.	10 mL
Flour tortillas (10 inch, 25 cm, size)	8	8
Salsa	1/2 cup	125 mL

Combine first 5 ingredients in medium bowl. Add beef strips. Stir to coat. Set aside.

(continued on next page)

104 Sandwiches

Sauté mushrooms, red pepper and green onion in cooking oil in frying pan for 2 to 3 minutes until liquid has evaporated. Transfer to medium bowl.

Wrap tortillas in foil. Heat in 350°F (175°F) oven for 8 to 10 minutes until warmed but soft.

Add beef strips with marinade to non-stick frying pan. Stir-fry for 5 minutes until browned. Add beef mixture to mushroom mixture. Toss. Place 1/2 cup (125 mL) beef mixture on each tortilla. Put 1 tbsp. (15 mL) salsa on top of each. Fold up, envelope-style, leaving top open. Makes 8 fajitas.

1 fajita: 242 Calories; 6.2 g Total Fat; 207 mg Sodium; 18 g Protein; 28 g Carbohydrate; 1 g Dietary Fiber

Pictured on page 125.

Corned Beef In Rye

Crunchy texture. Mild flavor. Ready in fifteen minutes.

Oblong rye loaf	16 oz.	454 g
Dijon mustard	2 tbsp.	30 mL
Finely chopped cabbage	2 cups	500 mL
Light salad dressing (or mayonnaise)	1/3 cup	75 mL
Granulated sugar	1 tsp.	5 mL
Lemon juice	1 tbsp.	15 mL
Medium red apple, with peel, cored and finely diced	1	1
Shaved corned beef	8 oz.	225 g
Grated Swiss cheese	1 cup	250 mL

Cut 2 inch (5 cm) horizontal slice from top of loaf. Hollow out bottom of loaf, leaving about 1/2 inch (12 mm) shell. Spread mustard on cut side of loaf top.

Combine cabbage, salad dressing, sugar, lemon juice and apple in medium bowl. Mix well.

Layer 1/3 of corned beef in shell. Top with 1/2 of cheese and 1/2 of cabbage mixture. Repeat with 1/3 of beef, 1/2 of cheese, 1/2 of cabbage mixture and top with remaining beef. Press top down. Wrap tightly in plastic wrap. Chill. Cuts into six 2 inch (5 cm) slices.

1 slice: 289 Calories; 13.3 g Total Fat; 688 mg Sodium; 14 g Protein; 31 g Carbohydrate; 2 g Dietary Fiber

Layered Italian Loaf

A make-ahead sandwich. Great for picnics!

Olive (or cooking) oil	1/3 cup	75 mL
Red wine vinegar	2 tbsp.	30 mL
Roma (plum) tomatoes, seeded and diced	4	4
Dried sweet basil	1 tbsp.	15 mL
Garlic cloves, minced (or 3/4 tsp., 4 mL, powder)	3	3
Jar of pimiento, with liquid, chopped	2 oz.	57 mL
Finely chopped green pepper	1/2 cup	125 mL
Finely chopped red pepper	1/2 cup	125 mL
Chopped pitted ripe olives	1/2 cup	125 mL
Round Italian bread loaf (10 inch, 25 cm)	1	1
Grated provolone cheese	1/2 cup	125 mL
Grated Swiss cheese	1/2 cup	125 mL
Deli (or cooked) lean beef, very thinly sliced	1/2 lb.	225 g

Combine first 9 ingredients in medium bowl. Cover. Marinate at room temperature for 1 to 2 hours.

Cut loaf in half horizontally. Hollow out halves, leaving 1 inch (2.5 cm) edge. Measure 3 tbsp. (50 mL) of juices from tomato mixture into small bowl. Brush over cut surface on both halves of loaf. Spread tomato mixture and remaining juices evenly over both halves.

Divide and sprinkle both cheeses over tomato mixture. Layer beef on bottom half only. Pack both fillings down slightly. Carefully turn top half onto bottom half. Firmly press top down on loaf. Wrap tightly in plastic wrap. Chill overnight with something heavy on top to keep loaf flattened. Cuts into 8 wedges.

1 wedge: 367 Calories; 15.7 g Total Fat; 520 mg Sodium; 18 g Protein; 38 g Carbohydrate; 2 g Dietary Fiber

1. Savory Rib Roast, page 88
2. Ruby-Glazed Roast Beef, page 91

Props Courtesy Of: The Bay

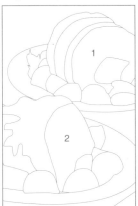

Sandwiches

Surprise Burgers

A nice mingling of flavors in the beef with a surprise in the middle!

Lean ground beef	1 lb.	454 g
Large egg	1	1
Chopped cooked spinach, squeezed dry	3 tbsp.	50 mL
Grated onion	1 tbsp.	15 mL
Salt	1/2 tsp.	2 mL
Freshly ground pepper, sprinkle		
Grated medium Cheddar cheese	3 tbsp.	50 mL
Light salad dressing (or mayonnaise), optional	3 tbsp.	50 mL
Ketchup (optional)	3 tbsp.	50 mL
Kaiser (or other) rolls, cut in half and toasted	4	4
Tomato slices	4	4

Combine first 6 ingredients in medium bowl. Divide mixture into 4 large portions and 4 small portions. Form large portions into patties. Make an indentation in center of each patty.

Fill each indentation with 1/4 of cheese. Flatten small portion of beef mixture. Place over patties. Pinch to seal. Broil or barbecue patties for 10 minutes until no longer pink inside.

Spread salad dressing and ketchup on each toasted roll. Top with patties and tomato. Makes 4 burgers.

1 burger: 445 Calories; 19.1 g Total Fat; 1013 mg Sodium; 29 g Protein; 38 g Carbohydrate; 1 g Dietary Fiber

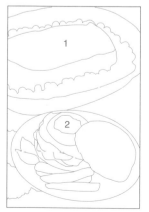

1. Cranberry Roast, page 93
2. Tangy Beef Roast, page 95

Props Courtesy Of: La Cache
Mystique

Pita Pizzas

Nice crunchy rim under mozzarella-covered mushrooms and green pepper. Yum!

Lean ground beef	1/2 lb.	225 g
Finely diced onion	1/3 cup	75 mL
Ground oregano	1/4 tsp.	1 mL
Salt	1/4 tsp.	1 mL
Garlic powder	1/4 tsp.	1 mL
Whole wheat pitas (7 inch, 18 cm, size)	8	8
Tomato (or pizza) sauce	7 1/2 oz.	213 mL
Finely chopped fresh mushrooms	1 cup	250 mL
Finely diced green pepper	1 1/2 cups	375 mL
Grated part-skim mozzarella cheese	2 cups	500 mL

Scramble-fry first 5 ingredients in non-stick frying pan until onion is soft and beef is no longer pink. Drain.

Flatten pitas using rolling pin. Place pitas on ungreased baking sheet. Spread each pita with about 1 1/2 tbsp. (25 mL) tomato sauce. Sprinkle each with 3 tbsp. (50 mL) beef mixture, 2 tbsp. (30 mL) mushrooms and 2 tbsp. (30 mL) green pepper. Sprinkle 1/4 cup (60 mL) cheese over top. Broil 6 to 8 inches (15 to 20 cm) from heat until edges are crusty and cheese is melted. To serve, cut into quarters. Makes 8 pita pizzas.

1 pizza: 313 Calories; 9 g Total Fat; 737 mg Sodium; 20 g Protein; 41 g Carbohydrate; 6 g Dietary Fiber

Pictured on page 125.

Mexican Flatbread Pizza

Brightly colored pizza with salsa-flavored and tenderized beef.

Flatbread (or pre-baked pizza crust), 12 inch (30 cm) size	1	1
MARINADE		
Chunky salsa	1/2 cup	125 mL
Lime juice	2 tbsp.	30 mL
Minute (or fast-fry) steaks, 1/4 inch (6 mm) thick	1 lb.	454 g

(continued on next page)

Sandwiches

Chunky salsa	1/2 cup	125 mL
Grated Monterey Jack cheese	1/4 cup	60 mL
Grated medium Cheddar cheese	1/4 cup	60 mL

Place flatbread on ungreased baking sheet. Warm in 250°F (120°C) oven while preparing steak.

Marinade: Combine first amount of salsa and lime juice in small bowl. Place steaks in shallow dish. Pour marinade over steak. Turn to coat. Cover. Marinate for 15 minutes. Remove steaks. Discard marinade. Cook steak in non-stick frying pan for 2 minutes per side until desired doneness. Cut into thin strips.

Remove flatbread from oven. Spread with second amount of salsa. Top with beef strips. Sprinkle with both cheeses. Broil for 2 minutes until cheese is melted. Cuts into 8 wedges.

1 wedge: 237 Calories; 7.3 g Total Fat; 560 mg Sodium; 18 g Protein; 24 g Carbohydrate; 1 g Dietary Fiber

Mexi-Beef Pitas

A great kids' lunch or after-school snack. Make the filling ahead and keep on hand.

Pitas (3 inch, 7.5 cm, size)	10	10
Lean ground beef	1 lb.	454 g
Finely chopped onion	1/2 cup	125 mL
Can of pinto beans, drained and rinsed	14 oz.	398 mL
Diced green pepper	1/2 cup	125 mL
Diced red pepper	1/4 cup	60 mL
Chili powder	2 tsp.	10 mL
Salt	1 tsp.	5 mL
Grated Monterey Jack cheese	3/4 cup	175 mL

Flatten pitas using rolling pin. Place pitas on ungreased baking sheet. Warm in 300°F (150°C) oven.

Scramble-fry ground beef in non-stick frying pan until no longer pink. Drain.

Add next 6 ingredients. Mix well. Heat thoroughly for 2 to 3 minutes. Remove pitas from oven. Make slit in seam of each pita. Spoon ground beef mixture into pitas.

Sprinkle with cheese. Place on ungreased baking sheet. Bake in oven until cheese is melted. Makes 10 mini-pita sandwiches.

1 pita sandwich: 182 Calories; 7 g Total Fat; 446 mg Sodium; 14 g Protein; 16 g Carbohydrate; 3 g Dietary Fiber

Beef Vegetable Sandwiches

A healthy tasting salad with a nice tang from the yogurt. Uses leftover cooked beef.

Plain yogurt	1/2 cup	125 mL
Grated carrot	1/2 cup	125 mL
Finely chopped onion	1 tbsp.	15 mL
Dried sweet basil	1/2 tsp.	2 mL
Kaiser (or other) rolls, cut in half	4	4
Iceberg lettuce leaves	4	4
Large tomato, thinly sliced	1	1
Cooked lean beef, thinly sliced	8 oz.	225 g
Medium cucumber, peeled and thinly sliced	1/2	1/2
Grated medium Cheddar cheese	1/4 cup	60 mL
Alfalfa sprouts	1 cup	250 mL
Salt, sprinkle		
Pepper, sprinkle		

Combine yogurt, carrot, onion, and basil in small bowl. Set aside.

Layer bottom halves of buns with lettuce, tomato, beef, cucumber, cheese and sprouts. Sprinkle with salt and pepper. Spoon 1/4 cup (60 mL) yogurt mixture over top of sprouts. Cover with top halves of buns. Makes 4 sandwiches.

1 sandwich: 300 Calories; 8.2 g Total Fat; 227 mg Sodium; 28 g Protein; 37 g Carbohydrate; 1 g Dietary Fiber

Pictured on page 125.

Beef And Avocado Sandwiches

Attractive layers of beef, lettuce and tomato with lovely basil and avocado flavors.

Fresh sweet basil, packed	1 cup	250 mL
Coarsely chopped fresh parsley, tough stems removed	1/4 cup	60 mL
Garlic cloves, halved	3	3
Coarsely chopped onion	1/4 cup	60 mL
Ripe avocado, peeled and halved	1	1
Lemon juice	2 tbsp.	30 mL
Salt	1/2 tsp.	2 mL
Freshly ground pepper, sprinkle		
Olive (or cooking) oil	3 tbsp.	50 mL

(continued on next page)

Italian (or kaiser rolls) buns, cut in half	8	8
Deli (or cooked) lean beef, very thinly sliced	1 lb.	454 g
Large tomatoes, sliced	2	2
Red (or green) leafy lettuce leaves	8	8
Salt, sprinkle		
Freshly ground pepper, sprinkle		

Combine basil, parsley, garlic and onion in food processor. Process, scraping down sides occasionally, until herbs are finely chopped.

Add next 5 ingredients. Process until smooth. Transfer mixture to medium bowl. Cover. Chill for 30 minutes to blend flavors.

Divide and spread avocado mixture among bottom halves of buns.

Layer beef, tomato and lettuce on top of avocado mixture. Sprinkle with second amounts of salt and pepper. Cover with top halves of buns. Makes 8 sandwiches.

1 sandwich: 356 Calories; 13.8 g Total Fat; 527 mg Sodium; 23 g Protein; 36 g Carbohydrate; 3 g Dietary Fiber

---

Gyro Sandwiches

A variation on a traditional Greek snack and a delicious change from an ordinary sandwich. The sauce is the perfect condiment for the filling.

GYRO SAUCE
Light salad dressing (or mayonnaise)	3/4 cup	175 mL
Milk	1/4 cup	60 mL
Garlic cloves, minced (or 1/2 tsp., 2 mL, powder)	2	2
Dried whole oregano	1 tsp.	5 mL
Pepper	1/4 tsp.	1 mL
Pitas (7 inch, 18 cm, size), cut in half	3	3
Deli (or cooked) lean beef, thinly sliced	3/4 lb.	340 g
Shredded iceberg lettuce	1 cup	250 mL
Chopped tomato	1 cup	250 mL
Thinly sliced red onion	1/2 cup	125 mL
Sliced pitted ripe olives	1/4 cup	60 mL

Gyro Sauce: Combine all 5 ingredients in medium bowl. Chill.

Fill pita pockets with beef, lettuce, tomato, onion and olives. Spoon about 2 1/2 tbsp. (37 mL) sauce into each pita pocket. Makes 6 pita pockets.

1 pita pocket: 287 Calories; 11.6 g Total Fat; 421 mg Sodium; 20 g Protein; 25 g Carbohydrate; 1 g Dietary Fiber

Minestrone

A nice blend of tomato and basil with a slight nip from the hot pepper sauce.

Lean ground beef	1 lb.	454 g
Garlic cloves, minced (or 3/4 tsp., 4 mL, powder)	3	3
Large onion, chopped	1	1
Large celery ribs, chopped	2	2
Water	6 cups	1.5 L
Beef bouillon powder	2 1/2 tbsp.	37 mL
Medium carrots, quartered lengthwise and sliced	2	2
Medium zucchini, with peel, quartered lengthwise and sliced	1	1
Bay leaves	2	2
Finely chopped fresh sweet basil (or 3 tsp., 15 mL, dried)	1/4 cup	60 mL
Dried whole oregano	1 tsp.	5 mL
Finely chopped fresh parsley (or 3/4 tsp., 4 mL, flakes)	1 tbsp.	15 mL
Pepper	1/4 tsp.	1 mL
Hot pepper sauce	1/2 tsp.	2 mL
Can of diced tomatoes, with juice	28 oz.	796 mL
Very small pasta (such as bow, alpha or orzo), uncooked	1 cup	250 mL
Can of kidney beans, with liquid	14 oz.	398 mL

Freshly grated Parmesan cheese, for garnish

Scramble-fry ground beef in large pot or Dutch oven until no pink remains. Drain.

Add garlic, onion, and celery. Sauté until onion and celery are soft.

Add next 11 ingredients. Stir. Bring to a boil. Reduce heat. Cover. Simmer for 45 minutes until vegetables are tender.

Add pasta and beans with liquid. Simmer, uncovered, for 10 minutes until pasta is tender. Remove and discard bay leaves.

Sprinkle individual servings with Parmesan cheese. Makes 13 cups (3.25 L).

1 cup (250 mL): 143 Calories; 3.5 g Total Fat; 528 mg Sodium; 10 g Protein; 18 g Carbohydrate; 4 g Dietary Fiber

Black Bean Soup

A very hearty winter soup with a lovely cumin and garlic flavor.
Excellent the next day.

Lean ground beef	1/2 lb.	225 g
Large onion, chopped	1	1
Garlic cloves, minced (or 3/4 tsp., 4 mL, powder)	3	3
Dried whole oregano	1/4 tsp.	1 mL
Dried thyme	1/4 tsp.	1 mL
Ground cumin	1/4 tsp.	1 mL
Cayenne pepper	1/4 tsp.	1 mL
Salt	1/2 tsp.	2 mL
Cans of black beans (19 oz., 540 mL, each), with liquid	2	2
Cans of condensed beef broth (10 oz., 284 mL, each)	2	2
Grated carrot	1/2 cup	125 mL
Water (1 soup can)	10 oz.	284 mL

Non-fat sour cream, for garnish
Finely diced red onion, for garnish

Scramble-fry ground beef, onion and garlic in large pot or Dutch oven until beef is no longer pink and onion is soft. Drain.

Add next 5 ingredients. Sauté for 2 minutes.

Combine beans with liquid and broth in blender or food processor. Purée until smooth. Pour into beef mixture. Add carrot and water. Bring to a boil. Reduce heat. Simmer, uncovered, for 10 minutes until carrot is soft and flavors are blended.

Garnish individual servings with swirls of sour cream and sprinkles of red onion. Makes 8 cups (2 L).

1 cup (250 mL): 211 Calories; 3 g Total Fat; 817 mg Sodium; 18 g Protein; 29 g Carbohydrate; 1 g Dietary Fiber

 All of the soups in this section can be frozen for up to 2 months. Cool soups completely before freezing. Fill containers, leaving about 1/2 inch (12 mm) of head space to allow for expansion. When ready to use, thaw, spoon off any fat and reheat, stirring often.

Oriental Beef And Cabbage Soup

Quick and easy soup with a nice nip.

Round steak, thinly sliced into 1/4 × 3/4 inch (0.6 × 2 cm) strips	3/4 lb.	340 g
Sherry (or alcohol-free sherry)	2 tbsp.	30 mL
Cooking oil	1 tbsp.	15 mL
Soy sauce	1 tbsp.	15 mL
Cornstarch	1/2 tsp.	2 mL
Cans of condensed beef broth (10 oz., 284 mL, each)	2	2
Water (2 soup cans)	20 oz.	568 mL
Ground ginger	1 tsp.	5 mL
Garlic powder	1/2 tsp.	2 mL
Freshly ground pepper	1/4 tsp.	1 mL
Coarsely shredded bok choy (or regular cabbage)	1 1/2 cups	375 mL
Chopped onion	1/2 cup	125 mL

Thinly sliced green onion, for garnish

Combine first 5 ingredients in small bowl. Set aside.

Combine broth, water, ginger, garlic powder and pepper in large pot or Dutch oven. Bring to a boil. Reduce heat. Simmer, uncovered, for 10 minutes.

Add bok choy and onion. Bring to a boil. Reduce heat. Simmer, uncovered, for 2 minutes. Add beef mixture. Simmer, uncovered, for 3 to 4 minutes until desired doneness.

Garnish individual servings with green onion. Makes 8 cups (2 L).

1 cup (250 mL): 94 Calories; 3.4 g Total Fat; 537 mg Sodium; 12 g Protein; 3 g Carbohydrate; trace Dietary Fiber

 Some garnishes work better than others for certain types of soup. Croutons and grated cheese are best in thicker soups while julienned vegetables and pasta work well in clear soups. Snipped fresh herbs can be used in all soups.

Meatball Vegetable Soup

Rich taste and a welcoming look.

Lean ground beef	1 lb.	454 g
Large egg	1	1
Dried whole oregano	1 tsp.	5 mL
Garlic clove, minced (or 1/4 tsp., 1 mL, powder)	1	1
Salt	1/2 tsp.	2 mL
Medium onion, thinly sliced	1	1
Cooking oil	1 tsp.	5 mL
Beef bouillon powder	2 tbsp.	30 mL
Boiling water	6 cups	1.5 L
Thinly sliced carrot	1/2 cup	125 mL
Thinly sliced celery	1/2 cup	125 mL
Chopped fresh parsley (or 3/4 tsp., 4 mL, flakes)	1 tbsp.	15 mL
Chopped fresh sweet basil (or 1/2 tsp., 2 mL, dried)	1 1/2 tsp.	7 mL
Worcestershire sauce	2 tsp.	10 mL

Salt, sprinkle
Pepper, sprinkle
Parmesan cheese, for garnish

Combine first 5 ingredients in large bowl. Shape into 1 inch (2.5 cm) balls. Brown on all sides in non-stick frying pan. Drain. Remove to medium bowl.

Sauté onion in cooking oil in same frying pan until soft and starting to brown.

Dissolve bouillon powder in boiling water in large pot or Dutch oven.

Add next 5 ingredients. Bring to a boil. Reduce heat. Add onion and meatballs. Cover. Simmer for 30 minutes until carrot and celery are tender.

Sprinkle with salt and pepper. Garnish individual servings with Parmesan cheese. Makes 8 cups (2 L).

1 cup (250 mL): 119 Calories; 6.2 g Total Fat; 671 mg Sodium; 12 g Protein; 3 g Carbohydrate; 1 g Dietary Fiber

Pictured on front cover.

Bok Choy Beef Soup

Dark and delicious.

Flank steak	1/2 lb.	225 g
Cornstarch	1 tsp.	5 mL
Freshly grated gingerroot (or 1/8 tsp., 0.5 mL, ground ginger)	1/2 tsp.	2 mL
Sesame (or cooking) oil	1/2 tsp.	2 mL
Soy sauce	1 tbsp.	15 mL
Dried crushed chilies, just a pinch		
Cans of condensed beef broth (10 oz., 284 mL, each)	3	3
Water	3 cups	750 mL
Julienned carrot	1 cup	250 mL
Finely slivered onion	1/2 cup	125 mL
Large ribs of bok choy, cut into 1/2 x 2 inch (1.2 x 5 cm) pieces	6	6
Thinly sliced green onion, for garnish		
Sesame seeds, toasted (see Tip, page 27), for garnish		

Slice steak with grain into 2 inch (5 cm) strips. Cut strips against grain into 1/8 inch (3 mm) slivers.

Combine cornstarch, ginger, sesame oil, soy sauce and chilies in small bowl. Add beef. Stir. Cover. Chill for 30 minutes.

Combine broth and water in large saucepan. Bring to a boil. Reduce heat. Add carrot and onion. Cover. Simmer for 15 minutes.

Stir in beef mixture and bok choy until boiling. Boil, uncovered, for 3 minutes.

Garnish individual servings with green onion and sesame seeds. Makes 8 cups (2 L).

1 cup (250 mL): 83 Calories; 3 g Total Fat; 894 mg Sodium; 10 g Protein; 4 g Carbohydrate; 1 g Dietary Fiber

Spicy Beef And Rice Soup

Lovely Mexican herb flavor with a touch of heat.

Minute steaks, cut into 1 inch (2.5 cm) cubes	1 lb.	454 g
Finely chopped onion	1/4 cup	60 mL
Garlic clove, minced (or 1/4 tsp., 1 mL, powder)	1	1
Cooking oil	2 tsp.	10 mL
Chopped fresh sweet basil (or 1 1/2 tsp., 7 mL, dried)	2 tbsp.	30 mL
Dried whole oregano	1/2 tsp.	2 mL
Dried thyme	1/4 tsp.	1 mL
Dried crushed chilies	1/4 tsp.	1 mL
Salt	1/2 tsp.	2 mL
Pepper	1/8 tsp.	0.5 mL
Water	5 cups	1.25 L
Can of diced Mexican-style stewed tomatoes, drained	14 oz.	398 mL
Long grain white rice, uncooked	1/2 cup	125 mL
Chili powder	1/4 tsp.	1 mL
Hot pepper sauce, to taste		
Chopped fresh cilantro (or fresh parsley)	2 tbsp.	30 mL

Sauté beef, onion and garlic in cooking oil in frying pan just until beef changes color.

Place beef mixture in medium bowl. Sprinkle with next 6 ingredients. Cover. Set aside.

Combine next 5 ingredients in large pot or Dutch oven. Bring to a boil. Reduce heat. Cover tightly. Simmer for 20 minutes.

Add beef mixture. Heat thoroughly. Gently stir in cilantro. Serve immediately. Makes 8 cups (2 L).

1 cup (250 mL): 157 Calories; 5.4 g Total Fat; 402 mg Sodium; 14 g Protein; 12 g Carbohydrate; trace Dietary Fiber

Steak Rubs

Double or triple your favorite rub recipe and keep a quantity handy in a closed container for quick and tasty steaks or burgers.

LEMON PEPPER RUB

Dried lemon peel	1 tsp.	5 mL
Garlic powder	1 tsp.	5 mL
Lemon pepper	1 tsp.	5 mL
Dried sweet basil	1/2 tsp.	2 mL

1 recipe: 19 Calories; trace Total Fat; 0.1 mg Sodium; 1 g Protein; 5 g Carbohydrate; trace Dietary Fiber

HERB AND SPICE RUB

Parsley flakes, crushed	1 tbsp.	15 mL
Paprika	1 tsp.	5 mL
Garlic powder	1 tsp.	5 mL
Pepper	1/4 tsp.	1 mL

1 recipe: 18 Calories; 0.4 g Total Fat; 3 mg Sodium; 1 g Protein; 4 g Carbohydrate; 1 g Dietary Fiber

CHILI RUB

Onion powder	1 tsp.	5 mL
Chili powder	1 tsp.	5 mL
Garlic salt	1 tsp.	5 mL
Dried whole oregano, crushed	1 tsp.	5 mL
Ground cumin	1 tsp.	5 mL

1 recipe: 33 Calories; 1.1 g Total Fat; 1219 mg Sodium; 1 g Protein; 6 g Carbohydrate; 1 g Dietary Fiber

NEW ORLEANS RUB

Garlic salt	1 tsp.	5 mL
Curry powder	1 tsp.	5 mL
Paprika	1 tsp.	5 mL
Cayenne pepper	1/4 tsp.	1 mL

1 recipe: 19 Calories; 0.6 g Total Fat; 340 mg Sodium; 1 g Protein; 4 g Carbohydrate; trace Dietary Fiber

Combine ingredients of one of above rubs in small cup. Rub on both sides of steaks, using heel of hand, or sprinkle on burgers. Use as little or as much rub as desired. Broil or grill steaks or burgers to desired doneness.

A Round Of Draft

Just the right amount of beer flavor with a tiny bit of sweetness.

BEER MARINADE

Can of beer	12 oz.	355 mL
Cooking oil	1/4 cup	60 mL
Apple cider vinegar	2 tbsp.	30 mL
Brown sugar, packed	2 tbsp.	30 mL
Medium onion, thinly sliced	1	1
Garlic cloves, minced (or 1/2 tsp., 2 mL, powder)	2	2
Bay leaf	1	1
Ground thyme	1/2 tsp.	2 mL
Salt	1/2 tsp.	2 mL
Freshly ground pepper	1/4 tsp.	1 mL
Round steak, 2 inches (5 cm) thick	3 lbs.	1.4 kg

Brown sugar, just a pinch

Beer Marinade: Combine first 10 ingredients in small bowl.

Place steak in shallow dish or resealable freezer bag. Pour marinade over steak. Turn to coat. Cover or seal. Marinate in refrigerator for 8 hours or overnight, turning several times. Remove steak, reserving marinade. Barbecue over high heat for 4 minutes per side. Reduce heat to medium. Barbecue by indirect cooking method (see page 10) for 20 minutes per lb. (45 minutes per kg.), brushing twice with reserved marinade, until desired doneness.

Remove onion from marinade. Remove and discard bay leaf. Sauté onion and brown sugar in non-stick frying pan until onion is soft. Pour in remaining marinade. Bring to a boil. Boil until reduced by 1/3. Cut steak across grain into 1/2 inch (12 mm) strips. Top with onion mixture. Serves 10.

1 serving: 223 Calories; 8.8 g Total Fat; 196 mg Sodium; 27 g Protein; 5 g Carbohydrate; trace Dietary Fiber

tip   *Cook an extra steak to use the next day, sliced, in a salad or sandwich.*

Teriyaki Steak

Quick, easy and so very tasty.

SAUCE

Soy sauce	1/4 cup	60 mL
Cooking sherry	2 tbsp.	30 mL
Granulated sugar	1 tbsp.	15 mL
Garlic clove, minced (or 1/4 tsp., 1 mL, powder)	1	1
Freshly grated gingerroot (or 1/8 tsp., 0.5 mL, ground ginger)	1/2 tsp.	2 mL
Pepper	1/4 tsp.	1 mL
Rib-eye (or sirloin) steak, 1 inch (2.5 cm) thick	1 1/2 lbs.	680 g

Sauce: Combine all 6 ingredients in small saucepan. Heat and stir until sugar is dissolved.

Brush both sides of steak with sauce. Place on rack in broiler pan. Broil steak for 5 to 6 minutes per side until desired doneness. Baste with sauce when steaks are turned. To serve, pour any remaining sauce over steak. Serves 6.

1 serving: 164 Calories; 6 g Total Fat; 742 mg Sodium; 22 g Protein; 3 g Carbohydrate; trace Dietary Fiber

Broiled Herbed Rouladen

Very eye appealing and a nice mustard flavor.

Dijon mustard	2 tbsp.	30 mL
Rouladen steaks (about 4 oz., 113 g, each) or top round slices (1/4 inch, 6 mm, thick)	2	2
Finely chopped fresh parsley (or 1 1/2 tsp., 7 mL, flakes)	2 tbsp.	30 mL

Spread mustard on 1 side of each steak. Sprinkle with parsley. Roll up, jelly roll-style. Secure with wooden picks. Place rolls on rack in broiler pan. Broil, seam side down, for 4 minutes. Turn and broil for 3 minutes. Do not overcook. Slice each roll into 1/4 inch (6 mm) slices. Serves 2.

1 serving: 142 Calories; 3.9 g Total Fat; 261 mg Sodium; 25 g Protein; 1 g Carbohydrate; trace Dietary Fiber

Pictured on page 126.

Pepper Steak For Two

Very mild pepper taste that may be accented with Salsa Romesco, page 15,
or Béarnaise Sauce, page 13.

Freshly ground black (or mixed) pepper	1 tsp.	5 mL
Round steak	1/2 lb.	225 g
Hard margarine (or butter)	2 tsp.	10 mL
Dry white (or alcohol-free) wine	1 tbsp.	15 mL
Worcestershire sauce	1 tsp.	5 mL
Garlic clove, minced (or 1/4 tsp., 1 mL, powder)	1	1
Celery salt	1/4 tsp.	1 mL

Rub pepper onto both sides of steak with heel of hand. Cut into 1/4 inch (6 mm) strips.

Melt margarine in frying pan. Add remaining 4 ingredients. Stir. Add beef. Heat and stir for about 3 minutes until desired doneness. Serves 2.

1 serving: 161 Calories; 6.6 g Total Fat; 300 mg Sodium; 22 g Protein; 2 g Carbohydrate; trace Dietary Fiber

Tenderloin With Mixed Peppercorn Sauce

Tenderloin is at its best if rare or medium rare. Do not overcook.

Tenderloin steaks (4 oz., 113 g, each)	4	4
Crushed whole mixed peppercorns	1 tsp.	5 mL
Cooking oil	2 tsp.	10 mL
Condensed beef broth	1/4 cup	60 mL
Gin	1 tbsp.	15 mL
Half-and-half cream	2 tbsp.	30 mL

Rub steaks with peppercorn. Heat cooking oil in frying pan until very hot. Sear steaks for 3 to 4 minutes per side until desired doneness. Remove steaks. Keep warm.

Pour broth and gin into frying pan. Simmer until reduced by 1/2.

Add cream. Simmer for 2 minutes. Serve over steaks. Serves 4.

1 serving: 204 Calories; 10.2 g Total Fat; 135 mg Sodium; 24 g Protein; 1 g Carbohydrate; trace Dietary Fiber

Pictured on page 143.

Steaks

Zesty Broiled Steak

Delicate orange flavor with a hint of soy sauce. Lovely combination.

Soy sauce	1 tbsp.	15 mL
Garlic clove, minced (or 1/4 tsp., 1 mL, powder)	1	1
Freshly grated orange peel	1 tsp.	5 mL
Dried rosemary, crushed	1/2 tsp.	2 mL
Sirloin (or rib-eye or strip loin) steak, 3/4 inch (2 cm) thick	1/2 lb.	225 g

Sesame seeds, for garnish

Combine soy sauce, garlic, orange peel and rosemary in small cup. Use all of soy sauce mixture to coat both sides of steak. Let stand for 10 minutes to absorb flavors. Place on rack in broiler pan. Broil for 4 to 6 minutes per side until desired doneness.

Sprinkle with sesame seeds. Serves 2.

1 serving: 142 Calories; 4.1 g Total Fat; 571 mg Sodium; 23 g Protein; 2 g Carbohydrate; trace Dietary Fiber

Pictured on page 126.

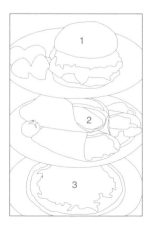

1. Beef Vegetable Sandwiches, page 112
2. Speedy Fajitas, page 104
3. Pita Pizzas, page 110

Props Courtesy Of: The Bay

Sesame Steak

Sesame and soy sauce are favorite flavors. Very pleasing.

MARINADE		
Cooking oil	1 tbsp.	15 mL
Soy sauce	1/3 cup	75 mL
Granulated sugar	1/4 cup	60 mL
Chopped green onion	1/4 cup	60 mL
Sesame seeds, toasted (see Tip, page 27)	2 tbsp.	30 mL
Garlic cloves, minced (or 3/4 tsp., 4 mL, powder)	3	3
Hot pepper sauce	1/8 tsp.	0.5 mL
Round (or cross-rib or boneless blade) steak, 1 inch (2.5 cm) thick	1 1/2 lbs.	680 g

Marinade: Combine first 7 ingredients in small bowl.

Place steak in shallow dish or resealable freezer bag. Pour marinade over steak. Turn to coat. Cover or seal. Marinate in refrigerator for at least 12 hours or overnight, turning several times. Remove steak. Discard marinade. Place steak on rack in broiler pan. Broil for 7 to 9 minutes per side until desired doneness. Serves 4.

1 serving: 206 Calories; 10 g Total Fat; 383 mg Sodium; 23 g Protein; 4 g Carbohydrate; trace Dietary Fiber

Pictured on page 143.

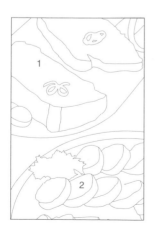

1. Zesty Broiled Steak, page 124
2. Broiled Herbed Rouladen, page 122

Props Courtesy Of: Le Gnome

Acapulco Beef Filet

Beef coated in a smooth, wonderful red sauce.

Large onion, cut lengthwise into slivers	1	1
Hard margarine (or butter)	1 tbsp.	15 mL
Red pepper, cut into 1 1/2 inch (3.8 cm) chunks	1	1
Yellow pepper, cut into 1 1/2 inch (3.8 cm) chunks	1	1
Chili sauce	3 tbsp.	50 mL
Condensed beef broth	1/2 cup	125 mL
Salt	1/2 tsp.	2 mL
Freshly ground pepper	1 tsp.	5 mL
Filet (or tenderloin) steaks (about 4 oz., 113 g, each)	4	4
Freshly ground pepper, sprinkle		
Cooking oil	1 tbsp.	15 mL
Tequila	2 tbsp.	30 mL
Lime juice	1 tbsp.	15 mL
Salt	1/4 tsp.	1 mL

Sauté onion in margarine in frying pan, stirring frequently, until golden.

Add both peppers. Sauté for 2 to 3 minutes. Add chili sauce, broth, first amounts of salt and pepper. Cover. Simmer for 7 minutes. Drain. Transfer to serving platter. Keep warm.

Blot steaks with paper towels. Rub second amount of pepper into both sides of steak with heel of hand.

Heat cooking oil in frying pan until very hot. Sear steaks for 3 to 4 minutes per side until desired doneness. Place steaks on top of warm pepper mixture.

Combine tequila and lime juice in cast iron frying pan. Simmer, uncovered, for 2 to 3 minutes. Sprinkle with second amount of salt. Pour sauce over steaks. Serves 4.

1 serving: 271 Calories; 13.7 g Total Fat; 768 mg Sodium; 25 g Protein; 7 g Carbohydrate; 1 g Dietary Fiber

Dijon Lemon Steak

Very nice mustard and lemon flavors are evident without being too strong.

MUSTARD SAUCE

Dijon mustard	3 tbsp.	50 mL
Lemon juice	1 1/2 tsp.	7 mL
Worcestershire sauce	1 tsp.	5 mL
Garlic clove, minced (or 1/4 tsp., 1 mL, powder)	1	1
Freshly ground pepper	1/2 tsp.	2 mL
Strip loin steak	1 lb.	454 g

Mustard Sauce: Combine mustard, lemon juice, Worcestershire sauce, garlic and pepper in small bowl.

Brush mustard mixture on both sides of steak. Place on rack in broiler pan. Broil for 5 to 6 minutes per side, brushing occasionally with mustard mixture, until desired doneness. Serves 4.

1 serving: 156 Calories; 6.1 g Total Fat; 225 mg Sodium; 23 g Protein; 1 g Carbohydrate; trace Dietary Fiber

Pictured on page 143.

Sweet And Sour Steak

Complement this dish with steamed rice or noodles.

Cooking oil	1 tsp.	5 mL
Eye of round (or sirloin tip) steak, cut into 4 pieces	1 lb.	454 g
SAUCE		
Sweet and sour barbecue sauce	1/2 cup	125 mL
Mild (or hot) chutney	1/4 cup	60 mL
Finely chopped onion	1/4 cup	60 mL
Soy sauce	1 tbsp.	15 mL

Heat cooking oil in frying pan until very hot. Sear steak quickly on both sides.

Sauce: Combine all 4 ingredients in small bowl. Spoon over steak. Simmer, uncovered, for 6 to 10 minutes, turning once, until desired doneness. Serves 4.

1 serving: 163 Calories; 4.4 g Total Fat; 593 mg Sodium; 23 g Protein; 7 g Carbohydrate; 2 g Dietary Fiber

Yorkshire Stew

A homespun meal — true comfort food. Will remind you of Yorkshire pudding.

All-purpose flour	1/4 cup	60 mL
Bottom round steak, trimmed of fat, cut into 1 inch (2.5 cm) cubes	2 lbs.	900 g
Medium onion, thinly sliced	1	1
Cooking oil	2 tsp.	10 mL
Medium fresh mushrooms, sliced	6	6
Can of condensed beef broth	10 oz.	284 mL
Dry red (or alcohol-free) wine	1/2 cup	125 mL
Salt	1/2 tsp.	2 mL
Pepper	1/4 tsp.	1 mL
Dried rosemary, crushed	1/4 tsp.	1 mL
Dried tarragon	1/4 tsp.	1 mL
Tomato paste	1 tbsp.	15 mL
Worcestershire sauce	1 tsp.	5 mL
Medium carrots, cut into 1 inch (2.5 cm) pieces	3	3
YORKSHIRE PUDDING		
Large eggs	2	2
Milk	1 cup	250 mL
All-purpose flour	1 cup	250 mL
Salt	1/2 tsp.	2 mL
Hard margarine (or butter)	2 tbsp.	30 mL

Measure flour into plastic bag. Add beef cubes, a few at a time. Shake to coat. Place beef on lightly greased baking sheet. Bake in 425°F (220°C) oven for about 10 minutes, stirring once, until browned.

Sauté onion in cooking oil in large pot or Dutch oven until soft.

Add mushrooms. Sauté for 3 to 4 minutes.

Add next 8 ingredients. Stir well. Add beef. Cover. Simmer for 1 hour.

Add carrot. Cook for 1 hour until beef is tender.

Yorkshire Pudding: Beat eggs in medium bowl until frothy. Stir in milk. Blend well.

Combine flour and salt in medium bowl. Stir in milk mixture until smooth.

(continued on next page)

Place margarine in ungreased 2 quart (2 L) casserole. Heat in 400°F (205°C) oven for 3 minutes until melted. Remove from oven. Immediately pour pudding mixture in. Using slotted spoon, carefully place stew in center of batter to within 1 inch (2.5 cm) of edge, reserving gravy. Bake, uncovered, for 30 minutes. Reheat gravy. Slowly pour over hot stew. Serve immediately. Serves 6.

1 serving: 418 Calories; 13.9 g Total Fat; 871 mg Sodium; 37 g Protein; 31 g Carbohydrate; 2 g Dietary Fiber

Porcupine Meatball Stew

Nice garlic flavor in the meatballs and the vegetables are tomato-based.

Lean ground beef	1 1/2 lbs.	680 g
Long grain white rice, uncooked	1/2 cup	125 mL
Garlic clove, minced (or 1/4 tsp., 1 mL, powder)	1	1
Salt	1 tsp.	5 mL
Pepper	1/2 tsp.	2 mL
Fine dry bread crumbs	1/3 cup	75 mL
Large egg, fork-beaten	1	1
Finely chopped onion	1/2 cup	125 mL
Tomato juice	3 cups	750 mL
All-purpose flour	2 tbsp.	30 mL
Brown sugar, packed	1 tbsp.	15 mL
Salt	1/2 tsp.	2 mL
Pepper	1/2 tsp.	2 mL
Medium carrots, thinly sliced	6	6
Medium potatoes, cut into 6 pieces each	4	4
Small onion, quartered	1	1
Bay leaf	1	1

Combine first 8 ingredients in medium bowl. Shape into 1 1/2 inch (3.8 cm) balls. Place in lightly greased medium roaster. Cover. Bake in 350°F (175°C) oven for 20 minutes.

Combine next 5 ingredients in small bowl. Pour 1/2 of tomato juice mixture over meatballs.

Add carrot, potato, onion and bay leaf. Stir gently. Pour remaining tomato juice mixture over all. Cover. Bake in 350°F (175°C) oven for 2 hours until rice and vegetables are tender. Remove and discard bay leaf. Serves 6.

1 serving: 439 Calories; 18.6 g Total Fat; 1290 mg Sodium; 27 g Protein; 41 g Carbohydrate; 4 g Dietary Fiber

Pasta And Stew

*This winning recipe has a mild beef and
tomato flavor with a colorful presentation.*

All-purpose flour	3 tbsp.	50 mL
Paprika	1 tsp.	5 mL
Salt	1 tsp.	5 mL
Freshly ground pepper	1/4 tsp.	1 mL
Round (or blade) steak, cut into 1 inch (2.5 cm) cubes	1 1/2 lbs.	680 g
Olive (or cooking) oil	2 tbsp.	30 mL
Garlic clove, minced (or 1/4 tsp., 1 mL, powder)	1	1
Medium onion, cut into large chunks	1	1
Chopped fresh thyme leaves (or 3/4 tsp., 4 mL, dried)	1 tbsp.	15 mL
Olive (or cooking) oil	1 tsp.	5 mL
Can of diced tomatoes, with juice	14 oz.	398 mL
Barbecue sauce	1/4 cup	60 mL
Cans of condensed beef broth (10 oz., 284 mL, each)	2	2
Bay leaf	1	1
Carrots, sliced coin size	4	4
Celery rib, sliced	1	1
Sliced fresh mushrooms	2 cups	500 mL
Rotelle (wagon wheel) pasta, uncooked	1 1/2 cups	375 mL

Combine flour, paprika, salt and pepper in plastic bag. Add beef cubes, a
few at a time. Shake to coat. Heat first amount of olive oil in large pot or
Dutch oven. Brown beef on all sides. Remove to medium bowl.

Sauté garlic, onion and thyme in second amount of olive oil until onion is
soft.

Add tomatoes with juice, barbecue sauce, broth and bay leaf. Mix well.
Add beef. Bring to a boil. Reduce heat. Cover. Simmer for 1 1/2 hours.

Add carrots. Cover. Simmer for 30 minutes.

Add celery, mushrooms and pasta. Cover. Simmer for 20 minutes until
vegetables and pasta are cooked. Remove and discard bay leaf. Serves 6.

*1 serving: 364 Calories; 10.7 g Total Fat; 1274 mg Sodium; 32 g Protein; 35 g Carbohydrate;
4 g Dietary Fiber*

Beef Bourguignonne

Very tender beef with a lovely wine flavor. Serve over hot cooked noodles.

All-purpose flour	1/4 cup	60 mL
Salt	1/4 tsp.	1 mL
Pepper	1/4 tsp.	1 mL
Round (or blade or sirloin) steak, cut into 3/4 inch (2 cm) cubes	2 lbs.	900 g
Dry red (or alcohol-free) wine	2 cups	500 mL
Can of condensed beef consommé	10 oz.	284 mL
Bay leaves	2	2
Garlic clove, minced (or 1/4 tsp., 1 mL, powder)	1	1
Sliced fresh mushrooms	2 cups	500 mL
Freshly ground pepper, sprinkle		
Cooking oil	1 1/2 tsp.	7 mL
Boiling water, to cover		
Baskets of tiny white pearl onions	2	2
Diagonally sliced carrot	3 1/2 cups	875 mL
Chopped fresh parsley (or 3 tsp., 15 mL, flakes)	1/4 cup	60 mL

Combine flour, salt and pepper in plastic bag. Add beef cubes, a few at a time. Shake to coat. Place beef in lightly greased roasting pan. Bake, uncovered, in 425°F (220°C) oven for 10 minutes, stirring once, until browned.

Add wine, consommé and bay leaves. Reduce temperature to 350°F (175°C). Cover. Bake for 2 to 2 1/2 hours.

Sauté garlic, mushrooms and pepper in cooking oil in frying pan until mushrooms are browned. Add to beef mixture.

Pour boiling water over onions in medium bowl to loosen skins. Drain. Rinse in cold water. Cut off ends. Peel onions. Add onions, carrot and parsley to beef mixture. Stir. Cover. Cook for 1 hour until beef and vegetables are tender. Remove and discard bay leaves. Serves 6.

1 serving: 288 Calories; 7 g Total Fat; 525 mg Sodium; 33 g Protein; 16 g Carbohydrate; 3 g Dietary Fiber

Curried Beef Stew

Rich fruity curry taste with a nice balance of fruit and spice.
The flavor is best if made the day before.

Medium apple, diced	1	1
Small onion, thinly sliced	1	1
Cooking oil	2 tsp.	10 mL
Curry powder	1 1/2 tsp.	7 mL
Granulated sugar	2 tsp.	10 mL
Ground cumin	1 tsp.	5 mL
Beef stew meat	1 lb.	454 g
Can of diced tomatoes, with juice	19 oz.	540 mL
Lemon juice	1 tbsp.	15 mL
Beef bouillon powder	1 tsp.	5 mL
Hot water	1/4 cup	60 mL
Raisins	1/3 cup	75 mL
Freshly grated gingerroot (or 1/8 tsp., 0.5 mL, ground ginger)	1/2 tsp.	2 mL
Salt	3/4 tsp.	4 mL
Pepper	1/4 tsp.	1 mL
Diced green pepper	1/3 cup	75 mL
Cold water	2 tbsp.	30 mL
Cornstarch	1 tbsp.	15 mL

Sauté apple and onion in cooking oil in large non-stick frying pan for about 3 minutes.

Add curry, sugar and cumin. Mix well. Transfer to small bowl.

Brown beef in same frying pan. Return apple mixture to frying pan.

Add next 8 ingredients. Stir well. Cover. Simmer for 45 minutes.

Add green pepper. Simmer for 10 minutes until beef is tender.

Stir water into cornstarch in small cup until smooth. Gradually stir into stew. Heat and stir until boiling and thickened. Serves 4.

1 serving: 242 Calories; 6.6 g Total Fat; 920 mg Sodium; 20 g Protein; 28 g Carbohydrate; 3 g Dietary Fiber

Hungarian Stew

Hungarian paprika gives warmth to this hearty comfort food.

All-purpose flour	1/4 cup	60 mL
Hungarian (or regular) paprika	2 tsp.	10 mL
Salt	1/4 tsp.	1 mL
Freshly ground pepper	1/2 tsp.	2 mL
Round (or sirloin or blade) steak, cut into 3/4 inch (2 cm) cubes	1 1/2 lbs.	680 g
Large onion, thinly sliced	1	1
Garlic cloves, minced (or 1/2 tsp., 2 mL, powder)	2	2
Large red pepper, cut into slivers	1	1
Caraway seed	1/8 tsp.	0.5 mL
Cooking oil	2 tsp.	10 mL
Condensed beef broth	1 1/2 cups	375 mL
Tomato paste	2 tbsp.	30 mL
Hungarian (or regular) paprika	2 tsp.	10 mL
Sliced carrot	2 cups	500 mL
Non-fat sour cream	1 cup	250 mL

Combine flour, first amount of paprika, salt and pepper in plastic bag. Add beef cubes, a few at a time. Shake to coat. Place beef in lightly greased roasting pan. Bake, uncovered, in 425°F (220°C) oven for 10 minutes, stirring once, until browned. Transfer to bowl.

Sauté onion, garlic, red pepper and caraway seed in cooking oil in large pot or Dutch oven for 5 minutes. Add beef. Stir.

Add next 4 ingredients. Stir. Bring to a boil. Reduce heat. Cover. Simmer for 1 hour until beef is tender. Remove from heat.

Gently stir in sour cream. Serves 6.

1 serving: 230 Calories; 6.1 g Total Fat; 524 mg Sodium; 27 g Protein; 17 g Carbohydrate; 2 g Dietary Fiber

 Brown beef cubes a few at a time. Crowding inside the pan causes beef to steam instead of brown.

Three Pepper Stir-Fry

*A bright combination of colors with just the
right balance of sauce, beef and peppers.*

Top round (or sirloin) steak, trimmed of fat	1 lb.	454 g
Garlic cloves, minced (or 1/2 tsp., 2 mL, powder)	2	2
Oyster sauce	2 tbsp.	30 mL
Cooking oil	1 tbsp.	15 mL
Cooking oil	1 tsp.	5 mL
Sesame (or cooking) oil	1 tsp.	5 mL
Medium green pepper, sliced diagonally into 1 x 2 inch (2.5 x 5 cm) chunks	1	1
Medium red pepper, sliced diagonally into 1 x 2 inch (2.5 x 5 cm) chunks	1	1
Medium yellow pepper, sliced diagonally into 1 x 2 inch (2.5 x 5 cm) chunks	1	1
Medium onion, cut into slivers	1	1
Celery ribs, cut into thin diagonal slices	2	2
Beef bouillon powder	1 tsp.	5 mL
Boiling water	1/2 cup	125 mL
Soy sauce	1 tbsp.	15 mL
Brown sugar, packed	1 tsp.	5 mL
Dried crushed chilies	1/4 tsp.	1 mL
Cornstarch	2 tsp.	10 mL

Cut steak lengthwise into 2 inch (5 cm) strips. Cut strips crosswise into 1/4 inch (6 mm) slices. Julienne strips lengthwise into thin strips.

Combine garlic and oyster sauce in large bowl. Place beef strips in shallow dish or resealable freezer bag. Pour marinade over beef. Stir or turn to coat. Cover or seal. Marinate in refrigerator for 1 hour.

Heat first amount of cooking oil in frying pan or wok. Add beef mixture. Stir-fry, uncovered, for 3 minutes until beef is no longer pink. Remove beef with slotted spoon to small bowl. Discard liquid.

(continued on next page)

Heat second amount of cooking oil and sesame oil in frying pan until very hot. Add next 5 ingredients. Toss. Stir-fry for 3 to 5 minutes. Add beef. Toss.

Combine remaining 6 ingredients in small cup until smooth. Gradually pour into center of frying pan. Heat and stir until boiling and thickened. Serves 4.

1 serving: 307 Calories; 14.7 g Total Fat; 1140 mg Sodium; 27 g Protein; 17 g Carbohydrate; 3 g Dietary Fiber

---

Thai Beef And Pasta

Not only quick to prepare, this has an appealing look and great flavor.

Vermicelli (or capellini), broken in half, uncooked	4 oz.	113 g
Sesame (or cooking) oil	1 1/2 tsp.	7 mL
Sirloin steak, cut across grain into thin strips (or beef stir-fry strips)	1 lb.	454 g
Garlic cloves, minced (or 1 tsp., 5 mL, powder)	4	4
Jalapeño peppers, seeded and finely chopped (see Note)	3	3
Oyster sauce	3 tbsp.	50 mL
Granulated sugar	1 tsp.	5 mL
Lemon pepper	1 tsp.	5 mL
Cooking oil	1 tbsp.	15 mL
Chopped fresh sweet basil (or 3 tsp., 15 mL, dried)	1/4 cup	60 mL
Chopped fresh mint leaves	1 tbsp.	15 mL
Coarsely chopped roasted salted peanuts	1 tbsp.	15 mL

Lemon slices, for garnish

Cook pasta according to package directions. Drain. Add sesame oil. Toss. Keep warm.

Combine next 7 ingredients in large bowl. Mix well. Heat non-stick frying pan or wok. Stir-fry beef mixture for 5 to 6 minutes until beef is no longer pink. Pour over pasta.

Sprinkle with basil, mint and peanuts.

Garnish with lemon slices. Serves 4.

1 serving: 343 Calories; 11.2 g Total Fat; 181 mg Sodium; 28 g Protein; 32 g Carbohydrate; 3 g Dietary Fiber

Note: Wear gloves when chopping jalapeño peppers and avoid touching your eyes.

Beef Vegetable Dinner

Looks appetizing with the variety of vegetables.
Chestnuts and pea pods add a nice crunch.

Cooking oil	2 tbsp.	30 mL
Sirloin steak, cut across grain into 1/4 x 2 inch (0.6 x 5 cm) strips	2 lbs.	900 g
Garlic cloves, minced (or 1/2 tsp., 2 mL, powder)	2	2
Freshly grated gingerroot (or 3/4 tsp., 4 mL, ground ginger)	1 tbsp.	15 mL
Thinly sliced celery, cut on diagonal	3 cups	750 mL
Large green peppers, cut into strips	2	2
Large onion, cut into wedges	1	1
SAUCE		
Can of condensed beef broth	10 oz.	284 mL
Can of Chinese straw mushrooms, with liquid	14 oz.	398 mL
Can of sliced water chestnuts, drained	8 oz.	227 mL
Fresh (or frozen, thawed) pea pods	6 oz.	170 g
Water	2 cups	500 mL
Soy sauce	2 tbsp.	30 mL
Fancy (mild) molasses	2 tbsp.	30 mL
Salt	1 tsp.	5 mL
Brown sugar, packed	1 tbsp.	15 mL
Cornstarch	1/2 cup	125 mL

Heat cooking oil in large frying pan or wok. Stir-fry beef strips, in
2 batches, for 5 minutes each until no longer pink. Transfer to large pot
or Dutch oven.

Add garlic, ginger, celery, green pepper and onion to same frying pan.
Stir-fry for 5 minutes. Add to beef.

Sauce: Combine all 10 ingredients in frying pan. Heat until bubbling. This
may have to be done in 2 batches. Pour over beef mixture. Stir. Heat
through. Serves 8.

1 serving: 270 Calories; 7.9 g Total Fat; 1031 mg Sodium; 26 g Protein; 23 g Carbohydrate;
3 g Dietary Fiber

Pictured on page 144.

Spicy Beef With Asparagus

A nice blend of flavors from the sesame oil and chilies.

Soy sauce	1 tbsp.	15 mL
Sesame (or cooking) oil	1 tbsp.	15 mL
Red wine vinegar	1 tbsp.	15 mL
Dried crushed chilies	1/4 tsp.	1 mL
Garlic clove, minced (or 1/4 tsp., 1 mL, powder)	1	1
Sirloin beef strips, 1/8 inch (3 mm) thick	1/2 lb.	225 g
Fresh asparagus, cut diagonally into 1 1/2 inch (3.8 cm) pieces	1/2 lb.	225 g
Water		
Beef bouillon powder	1 tsp.	5 mL
Cornstarch	2 tsp.	10 mL
Boiling water	1/2 cup	125 mL
Sesame seeds, toasted (see Tip, page 27), for garnish		

Combine first 5 ingredients in medium bowl. Place beef strips in shallow dish or resealable freezer bag. Pour marinade over beef. Stir or turn to coat. Cover or seal. Marinate for at least 1 hour. Remove beef, reserving marinade.

Cook or steam asparagus in medium saucepan with water for about 8 minutes until tender-crisp. Heat non-stick frying pan or wok. Stir-fry beef for about 3 minutes until no longer pink.

Stir bouillon powder and cornstarch into second amount of water and reserved marinade in small bowl until smooth. Gradually stir into beef. Heat and stir until boiling and thickened. Add asparagus. Stir to heat through.

Garnish with sesame seeds. Serves 2.

1 serving: 253 Calories; 11.7 g Total Fat; 896 mg Sodium; 28 g Protein; 10 g Carbohydrate; 2 g Dietary Fiber

 Because a wok has sloped sides and is deep, it requires less oil than a regular frying pan. If using a regular frying pan, more oil may have to be added to keep foods from sticking. Or use a frying pan with a non-stick coating.

Szechaun Beef

Crisp vegetables and tender beef with great Asian spiciness.

Top round (or sirloin) steak	1 lb.	454 g
MARINADE		
Finely chopped or grated gingerroot (or 1 1/2 tsp., 7 mL, ground ginger)	2 tbsp.	30 mL
Garlic cloves, minced (or 1/2 tsp., 2 mL, powder)	2	2
Chinese five-spice powder	1/2 tsp.	2 mL
Dried crushed chilies	1/4 tsp.	1 mL
Soy sauce	3 tbsp.	50 mL
Sherry	3 tbsp.	50 mL
Cooking oil	1 tbsp.	15 mL
Cooking oil	1 tsp.	5 mL
Julienned carrots	2 cups	500 mL
Julienned celery	1 cup	250 mL
Green onions, cut in 2 inch (5 cm) lengths and quartered lengthwise	8	8
Cold water	2 tsp.	10 mL
Cornstarch	2 tsp.	10 mL

Cut steak into 1/4 inch (6 mm) slices across grain and then cut each strip into 2 inch (5 cm) strips.

Marinade: Combine first 7 ingredients in small bowl. Place beef in shallow dish or resealable freezer bag. Pour marinade over beef. Stir or turn to coat. Marinate at room temperature for 1 hour.

Heat second amount of cooking oil in frying pan or wok. Stir-fry carrot, celery and green onion for 4 minutes until just tender-crisp. Add beef with marinade. Stir-fry for 3 minutes until beef is no longer pink.

Stir water into cornstarch in small cup until smooth. Gradually stir into beef mixture. Heat and stir until boiling and thickened. Serves 4.

1 serving: 241 Calories; 9 g Total Fat; 975 mg Sodium; 25 g Protein; 13 g Carbohydrate; 3 g Dietary Fiber

Pictured on page 144.

Stir-Fry Pasta And Beef

A quick dish. The perfect balance of vegetables,
beef and pasta with wonderful fresh ginger taste.

Vermicelli (or capellini or spaghettini), uncooked, broken in half	12 oz.	340 g
Beef bouillon powder	2 tsp.	10 mL
Boiling water	1 cup	250 mL
Freshly grated gingerroot (or 3/4 tsp., 4 mL, ground ginger)	1 tbsp.	15 mL
Garlic clove, minced (or 1/4 tsp., 1 mL, powder)	1	1
Soy sauce	3 tbsp.	50 mL
Cornstarch	1 tbsp.	15 mL
Sesame (or cooking) oil	1 tsp.	5 mL
Sirloin steak, cut across grain into thin strips	1 lb.	454 g
Medium carrots, thinly sliced	3	3
Sliced onion	1 cup	250 mL
Broccoli florets	2 cups	500 mL
Sliced mushrooms	1 cup	250 mL
Fresh pea pods	1 1/2 cups	375 mL
Fresh bean sprouts	2 cups	500 mL
Pepper, sprinkle		

Cook pasta according to package directions. Drain. Keep in cold water.

Combine next 6 ingredients in small bowl until smooth. Set aside.

Heat sesame oil in frying pan or wok. Add beef strips and carrot. Stir-fry for 2 minutes until beef is no longer pink.

Add next 4 ingredients and broth mixture. Stir-fry for about 2 minutes. Drain pasta. Add to beef mixture. Stir.

Add bean sprouts. Sprinkle with pepper. Stir until heated through. Serves 6.

1 serving: 416 Calories; 5.2 g Total Fat; 800 mg Sodium; 29 g Protein; 63 g Carbohydrate; 5 g Dietary Fiber

 Beef, raw or cooked, is much easier to slice thinly when partially frozen.

Spaghetti Stir-Fry

This wholesome, healthy dish is quick and simple with frozen vegetables.

Whole wheat (or regular) spaghetti, uncooked	12 oz.	340 g
Frozen Oriental (or Italian) mixed vegetables	3 cups	750 mL
Inside round (or sirloin tip) steak, cut across grain into thin strips	1 lb.	454 g
Chili sauce	2/3 cup	150 mL
Water	2 tbsp.	30 mL

Cook pasta according to package directions, adding frozen vegetables during last 5 minutes of cooking time. Drain well.

Heat non-stick frying pan or wok. Stir-fry beef for about 4 minutes until no longer pink.

Add chili sauce and water. Stir to heat through. Add drained spaghetti mixture. Toss to coat. Serves 6.

1 serving: 233 Calories; 3.8 g Total Fat; 86 mg Sodium; 22 g Protein; 31 g Carbohydrate; 1 g Dietary Fiber

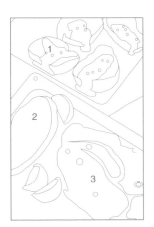

1. Tenderloin With Mixed Peppercorn Sauce, page 123
2. Dijon Lemon Steak, page 129
3. Sesame Steak, page 127

Props Courtesy Of: Libicz's Kitchen Essentials
Trail Appliances

Indian-Spiced Beef

Very colorful and very hot. The cumin and ginger are most noticeable.

Cooking oil	1 tbsp.	15 mL
Finely chopped gingerroot (3/4 tsp., 4 mL, ground ginger)	1 tbsp.	15 mL
Garlic cloves, minced (or 1/2 tsp., 2 mL, powder)	2	2
Medium onion, coarsely chopped	1	1
Ground cumin	1 tsp.	5 mL
Cooked lean beef, cut into 2 x 1/4 inch (5 x 0.6 cm) slices	2 cups	500 mL
Medium red pepper, cut into chunks	1/2	1/2
Medium yellow pepper, cut into chunks	1/2	1/2
Ripe large mango, diced	1	1
Dried crushed chilies	1/2 tsp.	2 mL
Medium tomato, chopped	1	1
Ground cardamom	1/4 tsp.	1 mL
Salt	1/4 tsp.	1 mL

Heat cooking oil in non-stick frying pan or wok. Add ginger, garlic, onion and cumin. Stir-fry for 2 minutes.

Add beef. Stir-fry for 1 minute.

Add remaining 7 ingredients. Stir-fry for 2 minutes until just heated through. Serve immediately. Serves 4.

1 serving: 219 Calories; 7.9 g Total Fat; 227 mg Sodium; 22 g Protein; 15 g Carbohydrate; 2 g Dietary Fiber

Pictured on page 54.

1. Beef Vegetable Dinner, page 138
2. Szechaun Beef, page 140

Props Courtesy Of: Le Gnome
                        Libicz's Kitchen Essentials

Spicy Beef And Broccoli

This excellent dish is everybody's favorite.

Egg white (large), fork-beaten	1	1
Cornstarch	1 tbsp.	15 mL
Sherry	1 tsp.	5 mL
Salt	1/2 tsp.	2 mL
Pepper	1/2 tsp.	2 mL
Hot pepper sauce	1/2 tsp.	2 mL
Top round (or flank) steak, cut across grain into thin strips	1 lb.	454 g
Soy sauce	1 tbsp.	15 mL
Chili sauce	1 tbsp.	15 mL
Red wine vinegar	1 tsp.	5 mL
Granulated sugar	1 tsp.	5 mL
Cooking oil	1 tbsp.	15 mL
Garlic cloves, minced (or 1/2 tsp., 2 mL, powder)	2	2
Sliced broccoli stems, cut diagonally very thin	1 1/2 cups	375 mL
Broccoli florets, sliced lengthwise	1 1/2 cups	375 mL
Sliced fresh mushrooms	1 cup	250 mL
Green onions, thinly sliced	4	4
Cooking oil	1 tbsp.	15 mL

Combine first 6 ingredients in medium bowl. Place beef in shallow dish or resealable freezer bag. Pour marinade over beef. Stir or turn to coat. Cover or seal. Marinate for at least 10 minutes.

Combine soy sauce, chili sauce, vinegar and sugar in small bowl. Set aside.

Heat first amount of cooking oil in frying pan or wok until hot. Stir-fry garlic and broccoli for 1 to 2 minutes until garlic is soft.

Add broccoli florets, mushrooms and green onion. Stir-fry for 4 to 6 minutes until broccoli is bright green and tender-crisp. Transfer to bowl.

Heat second amount of cooking oil in same frying pan. Stir-fry beef with marinade, in 2 batches, for 2 to 3 minutes. Return all beef to frying pan. Add chili sauce mixture. Heat and stir until bubbling. Stir in broccoli mixture. Cover. Simmer until heated through. Serves 4.

1 serving: 293 Calories; 15.5 g Total Fat; 697 mg Sodium; 29 g Protein; 9 g Carbohydrate; 2 g Dietary Fiber

Pineapple Beef Stir-Fry

This sweet and sour stir-fry is sure to please.

Flank steak	1 lb.	454 g
Cooking oil	1 tbsp.	15 mL
Medium onion, sliced lengthwise into 1 inch (2.5 cm) wedges	1	1
Can of pineapple chunks, with juice	14 oz.	398 mL
Brown sugar, packed	1/4 cup	60 mL
White vinegar	1/4 cup	60 mL
Chili sauce	2 tbsp.	30 mL
Soy sauce	1 tbsp.	15 mL
Water	2 tbsp.	30 mL
Cornstarch	2 tbsp.	30 mL
Medium red pepper, cut into 1 inch (2.5 cm) chunks	1	1
Medium tomatoes, cut into 8 wedges each	2	2

Cut steak with grain into 2 inch (5 cm) strips. Cut across grain into 1/8 inch (3 mm) slices.

Heat cooking oil in frying pan or wok. Add beef and onion. Stir-fry for 3 minutes until beef is no longer pink.

Add next 5 ingredients. Stir. Bring to a boil. Reduce heat. Cover. Simmer for 10 minutes.

Stir water into cornstarch in small cup until smooth. Gradually stir into beef mixture. Add red pepper and tomato. Heat and stir until boiling and thickened. Serves 6.

1 serving: 252 Calories; 8.1 g Total Fat; 219 mg Sodium; 18 g Protein; 28 g Carbohydrate; 2 g Dietary Fiber

Pictured on page 54.

 Stir-frying is a very fast cooking method. Have all ingredients measured and prepared before beginning, or prepare them in the morning and store, covered, in the refrigerator.

Beef And Greens Stir-Fry

Quick to prepare and quick to disappear.

Sirloin steak, cut across grain into thin strips	1 lb.	454 g
Garlic clove, minced (or 1/4 tsp., 1 mL, powder)	1	1
Freshly grated gingerroot (or 1/2 tsp., 2 mL, ground ginger)	2 tsp.	10 mL
Soy sauce	1 tbsp.	15 mL
Large onion, sliced lengthwise into 1 inch (2.5 cm) wedges	1	1
Sliced fresh mushrooms	3 cups	750 mL
Broccoli florets	3 cups	750 mL
Chicken bouillon powder	1 tsp.	5 mL
Cornstarch	2 tsp.	10 mL
Water	1/2 cup	125 mL
Green onions, sliced diagonally into 1 inch (2.5 cm) pieces	4	4
Chinese five-spice powder, just a pinch		

Heat non-stick frying pan or wok until hot. Add beef strips, garlic, ginger and soy sauce. Stir-fry for 2 minutes until beef is no longer pink.

Add next 3 ingredients. Stir-fry for 4 minutes until broccoli is tender-crisp.

Combine bouillon powder, cornstarch and water in small cup. Slowly stir into beef mixture until boiling and thickened.

Add green onion and five-spice powder. Stir-fry for 2 to 3 minutes. Serves 4.

1 serving: 187 Calories; 4.7 g Total Fat; 488 mg Sodium; 26 g Protein; 11 g Carbohydrate; 3 g Dietary Fiber

Pictured on page 54.

 Five-spice powder is an excellent blend of seasonings used in Chinese cooking to flavor red meats. It may contain star anise, anise seed, cloves, cinnamon, peppercorns, cardamom or orange peel and is available in the spice section of most grocery stores.

Beef With Zucchini Stir-Fry

Delicious crunchy stir-fry with a mild Chinese flavor.

Cornstarch	1 tbsp.	15 mL
Soy sauce	2 tbsp.	30 mL
Oyster sauce	1 tbsp.	15 mL
Granulated sugar	1/2 tsp.	2 mL
Freshly ground pepper, sprinkle		
Sesame (or cooking) oil	1/4 tsp.	1 mL
Top round (or flank or blade) steak, cut across grain into thin strips	3/4 lb.	340 g
Cooking oil	1 tbsp.	15 mL
Garlic cloves, minced (or 1/2 tsp., 2 mL, powder)	2	2
Medium carrot, sliced thinly on the diagonal	1	1
Medium onion, sliced lengthwise into slivers	1	1
Medium zucchini, sliced in half lengthwise, then on diagonal	1	1
Can of sliced water chestnuts, drained	8 oz.	227 mL
Frozen kernel corn	1 cup	250 mL

Salt, sprinkle
Pepper, sprinkle

Combine cornstarch, soy sauce, oyster sauce, sugar, pepper and sesame oil in small bowl. Place beef in shallow dish or resealable freezer bag. Pour marinade over beef. Stir or turn to coat. Cover or seal. Marinate for 15 minutes.

Heat cooking oil in frying pan or wok until hot. Add garlic. Stir-fry until golden. Add beef with marinade, carrot and onion. Stir-fry for 3 minutes.

Add zucchini, water chestnuts and corn. Stir-fry for 2 minutes. Cover. Cook for 3 minutes.

Sprinkle with salt and pepper. Serves 4.

1 serving: 273 Calories; 10.5 g Total Fat; 609 mg Sodium; 23 g Protein; 24 g Carbohydrate; 4 g Dietary Fiber

Measurement Tables

Throughout this book measurements are given in Conventional and Metric measure. To compensate for differences between the two measurements due to rounding, a full metric measure is not always used. The cup used is the standard 8 fluid ounce. Temperature is given in degrees Fahrenheit and Celsius. Baking pan measurements are in inches and centimetres as well as quarts and litres. An exact metric conversion is given below as well as the working equivalent (Metric Standard Measure).

Spoons

Conventional Measure	Metric Exact Conversion Millilitre (mL)	Metric Standard Measure Millilitre (mL)
1/8 teaspoon (tsp.)	0.6 mL	0.5 mL
1/4 teaspoon (tsp.)	1.2 mL	1 mL
1/2 teaspoon (tsp.)	2.4 mL	2 mL
1 teaspoon (tsp.)	4.7 mL	5 mL
2 teaspoons (tsp.)	9.4 mL	10 mL
1 tablespoon (tbsp.)	14.2 mL	15 mL

Cups

Conventional Measure	Metric Exact Conversion Millilitre (mL)	Metric Standard Measure Millilitre (mL)
1/4 cup (4 tbsp.)	56.8 mL	60 mL
1/3 cup (5 1/3 tbsp.)	75.6 mL	75 mL
1/2 cup (8 tbsp.)	113.7 mL	125 mL
2/3 cup (10 2/3 tbsp.)	151.2 mL	150 mL
3/4 cup (12 tbsp.)	170.5 mL	175 mL
1 cup (16 tbsp.)	227.3 mL	250 mL
4 1/2 cups	1022.9 mL	1000 mL (1 L)

Oven Temperatures

Fahrenheit (°F)	Celsius (°C)
175°	80°
200°	95°
225°	110°
250°	120°
275°	140°
300°	150°
325°	160°
350°	175°
375°	190°
400°	205°
425°	220°
450°	230°
475°	240°
500°	260°

Dry Measurements

Conventional Measure Ounces (oz.)	Metric Exact Conversion Grams (g)	Metric Standard Measure Grams (g)
1 oz.	28.3 g	28 g
2 oz.	56.7 g	57 g
3 oz.	85.0 g	85 g
4 oz.	113.4 g	125 g
5 oz.	141.7 g	140 g
6 oz.	170.1 g	170 g
7 oz.	198.4 g	200 g
8 oz.	226.8 g	250 g
16 oz.	453.6 g	500 g
32 oz.	907.2 g	1000 g (1 kg)

Pans

Conventional Inches	Metric Centimetres
8x8 inch	20x20 cm
9x9 inch	22x22 cm
9x13 inch	22x33 cm
10x15 inch	25x38 cm
11x17 inch	28x43 cm
8x2 inch round	20x5 cm
9x2 inch round	22x5 cm
10x4 1/2 inch tube	25x11 cm
8x4x3 inch loaf	20x10x7.5 cm
9x5x3 inch loaf	22x12.5x7.5 cm

Casseroles

CANADA & BRITAIN		UNITED STATES	
Standard Size Casserole	Exact Metric Measure	Standard Size Casserole	Exact Metric Measure
1 qt. (5 cups)	1.13 L	1 qt. (4 cups)	900 mL
1 1/2 qts. (7 1/2 cups)	1.69 L	1 1/2 qts. (6 cups)	1.35 L
2 qts. (10 cups)	2.25 L	2 qts. (8 cups)	1.8 L
2 1/2 qts. (12 1/2 cups)	2.81 L	2 1/2 qts. (10 cups)	2.25 L
3 qts. (15 cups)	3.38 L	3 qts. (12 cups)	2.7 L
4 qts. (20 cups)	4.5 L	4 qts. (16 cups)	3.6 L
5 qts. (25 cups)	5.63 L	5 qts. (20 cups)	4.5 L

Photo Index

Tip Index

Recipe Index

153

154

Feature Recipe from

Asian Cooking

New March 1, 2002

Asian Cooking offers recipes with unique flavors, brilliant colors and pleasing textures. These enticing dishes reflect influences from China, India, Indonesia, Japan, Korea, Malaysia, Philippines, Thailand and Vietnam.

Coco-Milk Chicken

This Indonesian dish has a smooth exceptional taste. Serve over rice.

Whole chicken, skin removed and cut into serving size pieces	3 lbs.	1.4 kg
Cooking oil	2 tbsp.	30 mL
Garlic cloves, minced (or 3/4 tsp., 4 mL, powder)	3	3
Finely chopped gingerroot (or 3/4 tsp., 4 mL, ground ginger)	1 tbsp.	15 mL
Medium onion, thinly sliced	1	1
Small red chili pepper, minced	1	1
Ground coriander	3/4 tsp.	4 mL
Coconut milk	2 cups	500 mL
Salt	1/2 tsp.	2 mL
Pepper (white is best)	1/4 tsp.	1 mL
Cashews, coarsely chopped	1/2 cup	125 mL

Fry chicken in cooking oil in frying pan for about 20 minutes, turning over once, until browned. Transfer to large plate. Cover. Keep warm.

Sauté next 5 ingredients in same frying pan for about 3 minutes until onion is soft and starting to turn golden.

Add coconut milk, salt and pepper. Stir. Simmer, uncovered, for 10 minutes. Add chicken. Cover. Simmer for about 45 minutes, turning chicken over once, until chicken is tender and no longer pink inside.

Sprinkle with cashews. Serves 4.

1 serving: 616 Calories; 46 g Total Fat; 443 mg Sodium; 41 g Protein; 14 g Carbohydrate; 1 g Dietary Fiber

Company's Coming cookbooks are available at **retail locations** throughout Canada!

See mail order form

Buy any 2 cookbooks—choose a 3rd FREE of equal or less value than the lowest price paid.   *Available in French

Original Series		CA$14.99 Canada		US$10.99 USA & International	
CODE		**CODE**		**CODE**	
SQ	150 Delicious Squares*	PI	Pies*	ST	Starters*
CA	Casseroles*	LR	Light Recipes*	SF	Stir-Fry*
MU	Muffins & More*	PR	Preserves*	MAM	Make-Ahead Meals*
SA	Salads*	LCA	Light Casseroles*	PB	The Potato Book*
AP	Appetizers	CH	Chicken*	CCLFC	Low-Fat Cooking*
DE	Desserts	KC	Kids Cooking	CCLFP	Low-Fat Pasta*
SS	Soups & Sandwiches	BR	Breads*	AC	Appliance Cooking*
CO	Cookies*	ME	Meatless Cooking*	CFK	Cook For Kids
VE	Vegetables	CT	Cooking For Two*	SCH	Stews, Chilies & Chowders
MC	Main Courses	BB	Breakfasts & Brunches*	FD	Fondues
PA	Pasta*	SC	Slow Cooker Recipes*	CCBE	The Beef Book
CK	Cakes	PZ	Pizza*	ASI	Asian Cooking ◀NEW▶
BA	Barbecues*	ODM	One Dish Meals*		*March 1/02*

Greatest Hits		CA$12.99 Canada		US$9.99 USA & International	
CODE		**CODE**		**CODE**	
BML	Biscuits, Muffins & Loaves*	SAS	Soups & Salads*	ITAL	Italian
DSD	Dips, Spreads & Dressings*	SAW	Sandwiches & Wraps*	MEX	Mexican

Lifestyle Series		CA$16.99 Canada	US$12.99 USA & International
CODE			
GR	Grilling*		
DC	Diabetic Cooking*		

Special Occasion Series		CA$19.99 Canada		US$19.99 USA & International
CODE		**CODE**		
CE	Chocolate Everything*	CFS	Cooking for the Seasons ◀NEW▶	
GFK	Gifts from the Kitchen		*April 1/02*	

Company's Coming COOKBOOKS

www.**companys**coming.com
visit our web-site

COMPANY'S COMING PUBLISHING LIMITED
2311 - 96 Street
Edmonton, Alberta, Canada T6N 1G3
Tel: (780) 450-6223 Fax: (780) 450-1857

Exclusive Mail Order Offer

See page 158 for list of cookbooks

Buy **2** Get **1** FREE!

Buy any 2 cookbooks—choose a 3rd FREE of equal or less value than the lowest price paid.

Quantity	Code	Title	Price Each	Price Total
			$	$
		don't forget		
		to indicate your		
		free book(s).		
		(see exclusive mail order		
		offer above)		
		please print		

| | TOTAL BOOKS (including FREE) | TOTAL BOOKS PURCHASED: | $ | |

	International		Canada & USA	
Plus Shipping & Handling (per destination)	$7.00	(one book)	$5.00	(1-3 books)
Additional Books (including FREE books)	$	($2.00 each)	$	($1.00 each)
Sub-Total	$		$	
Canadian residents add G.S.T(7%)			$	
TOTAL AMOUNT ENCLOSED	$		$	

The Fine Print

- Orders outside Canada must be **PAID IN US FUNDS** by cheque or money order drawn on Canadian or US bank or by credit card.
- Make cheque or money order payable to: **COMPANY'S COMING PUBLISHING LIMITED**.
- Prices are expressed in Canadian dollars for Canada, US dollars for USA & International and are subject to change without prior notice.
- Orders are shipped surface mail. For courier rates, visit our web-site: **www.companyscoming.com** or contact us: **Tel: (780) 450-6223 Fax: (780) 450-1857**.
- Sorry, no C.O.D's.

Gift Giving

- Let us help you with your gift giving!
- We will send cookbooks directly to the recipients of your choice if you give us their names and addresses.
- Please specify the titles you wish to send to each person.
- If you would like to include your personal note or card, we will be pleased to enclose it with your gift order.
- Company's Coming Cookbooks make excellent gifts: Birthdays, bridal showers, Mother's Day, Father's Day, graduation or any occasion...collect them all!

☐ MasterCard ☐ VISA

_____ Expiry date

Account # _____

Name of cardholder _____

Cardholder's signature _____

Shipping Address

Send the cookbooks listed above to:

Name: _____

Street: _____

City: _____ Prov./State: _____

Country: _____ Postal Code/Zip: _____

Tel: ( ) _____

E-mail address: _____

☐ YES! Please send a catalogue

Please mail or fax to:

Company's Coming Publishing Limited
2311 - 96 Street
Edmonton, Alberta, Canada   T6N 1G3
Fax: (780) 450-1857

Name:_____

Address:_____

_____

e-mail:_____

Reader Survey

We welcome your comments and would love to hear from you.
Please take a few moments to give us your feedback.

1. *Approximately what percentage of the cooking do you do in your home?*_____ %

2. *How many meals do you cook in your home in a typical week?*   _____

3. *How often do you refer to a cookbook (or other source) for recipes?*

☐ Everyday   ☐ 2 or 3 times a month   ☐ A few times a year
☐ A few times a week   ☐ Once a month   ☐ Never

4. *What recipe features are most important to you? Rank 1 to 7;*
   (1 being most important, 7 being least important).

_____ Recipes for everyday cooking
_____ Recipes for guests and entertaining
_____ Easy recipes; quick to prepare, with everyday ingredients
_____ Low-fat or health-conscious recipes
_____ Recipes you can trust to work
_____ Recipes using exotic ingredients
_____ Recipes using fresh ingredients only

5. *What cookbook features are most important to you? Rank 1 to 6;*
   (1 being most important, 6 being least important).

_____ Lots of color photographs of recipes
_____ "How-to" instructions or photos
_____ Helpful hints & cooking tips
_____ Lay-flat binding (coil or plastic comb)
_____ Well organized with complete index
_____ Priced low

6. *How many cookbooks have you purchased in the last year?*_____

7. *Of these, how many were gifts?*_____

8. *Age group*

☐ Under 18   ☐ 25 to 34   ☐ 45 to 54   ☐ 65+
☐ 18 to 24   ☐ 35 to 44   ☐ 55 to 64

9. *What do you like best about Company's Coming Cookbooks?*

_____

_____

10. *How could Company's Coming Cookbooks be improved?*

_____

_____

11. *Topics you would like to see published by Company's Coming:*

_____

_____

Thank you for sharing your views. We truly value your input.

CCBE1